Equality in Action

Mee-Yan Cheung-Judge was a university teacher in the USA. She has a Ph.D. in Sociology. After moving to Britain she worked in grass-roots community development and on equal opportunities with voluntary organisations. In 1986 she set up Quality and Equality Organisation Development Consultancy and Training Services (Q & E) based in Oxford. Since then she has worked with over 120 organisations in the voluntary, public and private sectors using organisational development methods to work on various areas including equal opportunities, human resource development, management development and major change programmes.

Alix Henley is a freelance writer, researcher and consultant who has worked on various projects with Q & E over the last eight years. She specialises in matters to do with equal opportunities, health care and communication. She has published several books and training packages, including *Health Care in Multiracial Britain* (co-authored), *Caring in a Multiracial Society*, and, most recently, an Open College workbook on equal opportunities for health service managers. She is living temporarily in Switzerland.

NCVO — voice of the voluntary sector

NCVO champions the cause of the
voluntary sector. It believes that the
voluntary sector enriches society and
needs to be promoted and supported. It
works to improve its effectiveness,
identify unmet needs and encourage
initiatives to meet them.

Established in 1919 as the
representative body for the voluntary
sector in England, NCVO now gives
voice to some 600 national
organisations—from large 'household
name' charities to small self-help
groups involved in all areas of
voluntary and social action. It is also in
touch with thousands of other
voluntary bodies and groups, and has
close links with government
departments, local authorities, the
institutions of the European Union and
the business sector.

Equality in Action

Introducing Equal Opportunities in Voluntary Organisations

Mee-Yan Cheung-Judge and
Alix Henley

NCVO Publications

Published by NCVO Publications
(incorporating Bedford Square Press)
imprint of the National Council for Voluntary Organisations
Regent's Wharf, 8 All Saints Street, London N1 9RL

First published 1994

Typeset by GCS, Leighton Buzzard, Beds.
Printed in Great Britain by The Lavenham Press, Suffolk.

A catalogue record for this book is available from the British Library.

ISBN 0 7199 1415 9

Contents

v

List of Charts, Figures and Exercises

Exercises

Foreword

The 1990s has been characterised as the decade of equal opportunities in Britain, and yet the reality of the experience of many women and ethnic minorities in Britain is of a society which has not delivered equality despite the existence of race relations and sex discrimination legislation. It often seems as if nothing has changed, but there *have* been some far-reaching economic and social changes.

We have seen the growth of casualisation and fragmentation in the labour market, continuing high levels of unemployment within some ethnic minority communities and the continuing effects of economic recession.

There have also been other changes: increasing numbers of women in the labour market, many of them working part-time, structural changes in the public sector as a result of compulsory competitive tendering and market testing, and a refocusing on the need to deliver quality services to Britain's diverse communities. While these changes have had the effect of forcing the pace of organisational change, there has been a great deal of rhetoric in some organisations and little action. How do organisations translate the principles of social justice and equality into organisational values and practises which deliver equality?

This book is about that. It is important for equal opportunities because it goes beyond the rhetoric and is about equal opportunities practice. It is about going beyond commitment to practical implementation. Fundamentally, it is about organisational change and how to achieve it.

In many ways there has been a failure at national level to keep equality as a central feature of public policy debate and development, and when the achievement of equality has been on the agenda it has often been as part of a discussion of the need to have more women and those from ethnic minorities in positions of power and influence in British society. But on its own this will not deliver equality.

What is required is a strategic approach, at different levels of society. Every individual has to recognise that they have an important part to play. There are, of course, some key players. Voluntary organisations are important not just as employers, but as service providers and as institutions which have a 'values' framework. They must be seen to be operating good personnel policies and practices, and they have a role to play at the leading edge of change.

Many organisations in the voluntary sector have had to face severe financial difficulties in the last few years, and it has often been a struggle to stay in existence. Those that have sought to do that and at the same time grapple with the best ways of achieving quality and equality through organisational development are to be commended. The attainment of equality can seem like a far-reaching goal or an expedient principle, but it is, of course, best achieved by being at the core of organisational development and change. It is not a comfortable process, but it is one which delivers long-term and lasting results.

This book helps to achieve that and should be required reading not just within the voluntary sector, but in other areas.

Valerie Amos
Herman Ouseley

Preface

Where are we now?

Three decades have passed since the first British legislation on equality issues, the Race Relations Act. Further legislation has followed, dealing with discrimination against black and ethnic minority groups, women, and disabled people, all affecting voluntary organisations. Other groups, such as gay men and lesbians, though not protected by the law, have been active in campaigning for their rights.

The impetus began by the legislation has led many funding bodies to exert pressure on the voluntary sector by making an equal opportunities policy a condition for receiving grants. This pressure, together with campaigning activity by various minorities, has made equality one of the most important and controversial political issues on the agenda of the voluntary sector.

Many voluntary organisations have attempted to implement equal opportunities policies, particularly in employment and service delivery. Enormous amounts of energy, time and money have been expended. But, although there have been some notable successes (of which some examples are quoted in this book), more often the results have been conflict and disillusionment. Despite great and often painful effort, there has been little real progress towards genuine equality. Diverse user groups are still rarely represented, especially on management committees; the profiles of members, volunteers and staff, particularly at senior levels, have changed little; services are still mainly available to the 'traditional' pool of clients; the cultures of most voluntary organisations do not incorporate equality. Even those organisations that have made some progress are often still struggling with equal opportunities *intentions* rather than *actions*. And most people in the voluntary sector are still asking 'Why equal opportunities?' rather than 'When?' or 'How?'. As market forces and demands for value for money and the 'enterprise spirit' press increasingly on the voluntary sector, there is a real danger that equal opportunities issues will be squeezed out.

This depressing situation has grave implications, since the issue of equal opportunities is crucial for individuals, for organisations, and for society as a whole. It is an issue which voluntary organisations in particular, founded on principles of social justice, cannot afford to ignore in anything they do, especially in this time of shrinking resources. Without an equal opportunities policy, properly implemented as part of good overall management, no voluntary organisation can be sure that it is responding properly to the needs of all its clients or members, or that it is making full use of the pool of talents available to it among its staff and/or volunteers.

Aims, approach and content of this book

This book examines the difficulties that voluntary and other organisations have experienced up to now in attempting to implement equal opportunities policies. It discusses what has gone wrong and the lessons that can be learnt. It marks the shedding of old ideas about equal opportunities, for example that equal opportunities is purely a political issue, that it is an optional extra in a well-run organisation, or that it can be dealt with easily and superficially. Twenty years of experience confirm that these approaches to equal opportunities do not work and are often counterproductive.

Inequality is endemic in the voluntary sector as elsewhere in our society; reversing inequality involves fundamental re-thinking and change in any organisation. It requires clear analysis, detailed planning, a good deal of time and effort, and the commitment and involvement of key people at all levels. At the same time, for the organisation itself, achieving genuine equality in everything it does is absolutely vital in enabling it to do what it exists to do.

Within this book are three interwoven strands:

- the theory and technical basis of equal opportunities

- practical steps and ideas for achieving change based on organisational development methods

- case studies and examples.

The 'how' of good equal opportunities practice, rather than the ideological debate, is emphasised. The practical information and exercises this book contains will enable you to integrate equal opportunities into your organisation's aims and objectives, to visualise what your organisation will be like when it is a genuine equal opportunities organisation, to think through and plan the steps needed to reach that stage, to decide how to consult and work with key groups, and to review and monitor progress. The final chapter discusses how to create the kind of creative organisation in which equality can flourish.

Although this book provides you with the ideas and the thinking you need to achieve this major piece of change in your organisation, it does not tell you, for example, what your equal opportunities policy or codes of practice should say, provide the content of any workshops or training sessions you need to run, or list what you should include in your equality audit of services. A key principle of this book, and of the organisational development approach in general, is that every organisation is unique and needs different specific interventions to enable it and the people within it to achieve successful major change. The Further Reading section lists books and other materials which may be helpful on specific practical topics.

This book applies tried and tested organisational development methods (outlined in chapter 1) and is based on extensive experience of helping voluntary, public and private sector organisations to implement equal opportunities policies, particularly in the area of race. The basis of organisational development is the belief that it is important that *change* should always be *development*, that is, a positive force, and that it should always enable an organisation to move forwards and become stronger and healthier. Too often the implementation of equal opportunities has moved organisations backwards rather than forwards, and left them weakened and distressed.

It is important to note that although this book concentrates on the practical and positive aspects of change, it in no way denies the ugliness and complete unacceptability of discrimination in all its forms. However, the passion and polemic, which make us effective as political activists and advocates with society, are usually far less effective within organisations. Planned strategic methods of change, using organisational development techniques, work much better.

Who is this book for?

This book is for you if you want to know how you can make equal opportunities a reality in the voluntary organisation in which you are involved. You may, for example, be a manager, a member of staff, a volunteer, a member, a client, or a trainer (internal or external). You may be involved with a voluntary organisation that already has an equal opportunities policy or is implementing one, but which is having problems or wants to clarify certain issues.

You can use this book in several ways:

- If you are in a position to help introduce and implement an equal opportunities policy in your organisation, you can work through the book with colleagues, doing the exercises and developing a coherent and effective plan of action. In chapter 2 we discuss setting up a task group to take an organisation through the whole equal opportunities implementation process.

- If your organisation has already attempted to implement equal opportunities, you can use the book, alone or with other people, to review progress, using whichever exercises are appropriate to analyse problems and to work out what you need to do next.

- If you simply want to understand more about equal opportunities and how to implement it successfully, you can study the book alone or with others. This will enable you to be far clearer and stronger on such issues wherever and whenever they come up.

- If you want to understand more about the process of change in general within organisations and how to manage it successfully, this book provides an outline of the key ideas and practices involved, illustrated with reference to equal opportunities.

However you plan to use the book, we recommend that you begin by reading it through so that you understand the whole process before focusing on any one part.

Most of the exercises are applicable to both the public and private sectors, so this book may be used by *anyone* who is concerned to implement equal opportunities effectively in their organisation. It is also relevant for those involved in organisational training, or those running management or business studies courses, since an understanding of equal opportunities and equal opportunities management skills is vital for all managers.

We hope you will enjoy the process of exploration and development into which this book will take you and your organisation. We also hope that you will share in the excitement to be gained from helping organisations to develop and renew themselves and to become better fitted to face the challenges of today. This is an important opportunity to stand up and change things for the betterment of humanity. Take it, enjoy it and celebrate it!

Acknowledgements

This book is based largely on the work that Mee-Yan and Q & E (Quality and Equality Organisation Development Consultancy and Training Services) have carried out with clients in the voluntary sector over several years. The rich knowledge and experience gained through working with these voluntary sector clients, particularly on equal opportunities issues, have been invaluable and we should like to thank them all. Without them this book could not exist. In particular, we should like to thank those organisations which have so helpfully and willingly allowed us to use their experiences as case studies in this book, and which have helped us to put them together and make sure that they were accurate.

We should also like to thank Adah Kay, director of Family Service Units, for her practical support and encouragement, and Stephen Pittam, the assistant trust secretary of the Joseph Rowntree Charitable Trust, for his warm and kind support, his faith in times of difficulty, and his cheerfulness and willingness to listen. We should like to thank the Joseph Rowntree Charitable Trust for giving us a generous grant towards the work on this book. We should also like to thank Jackie Sallon, managing editor at NCVO Publications, for her publishing support.

We should like to give special thanks to Wendy van den Broek, the office manager at Q & E, for her amazingly patient administrative support and for managing the complexities of an international writing partnership, and Deepak Shenoy and Justin Hutchence at Q & E for their work on the graphics. We should like to thank Paddy O'Brien for carrying out most of the interviews for the case studies.

Finally, we should like to thank our families for bearing with us, supporting us while the pressure was on, and putting up with temporary neglect. Alix would particularly like to thank her mother, Lotti Henley, who stepped in and took over children and household in order that this book could be written.

Chapter 1
Introduction

This chapter sets out the basic facts about equal opportunities and its significance for the voluntary sector. It also outlines the organisational development approach and why it is effective in managing the change to equal opportunities.

Equal opportunities and the voluntary sector

Voluntary organisations play a vital role in British society: as providers of care and other services, as campaigners, as advocates, as empowerers and enablers. Central to all is a belief in social justice, of which equal opportunities is a part.

Most voluntary organisations provide special services or services that are not available from any other source. Often these are intended for the most disadvantaged members of society. It is therefore doubly important that these services reach those who need them most, and that no one is denied access because of conscious or unconscious discrimination, or simply because the organisation has failed to recognise and meet new demands and circumstances. The aim of an equal opportunities policy is to ensure that everyone, and particularly members of those groups most likely to experience discrimination and disadvantage, has fair and full access to services.

In their campaigning and advocacy activities, voluntary organisations often work with and for those groups to whom a voice and a fair share in the benefits of society are denied. The views and needs of these groups must be accurately represented and properly heard.

Voluntary organisations also have a key role in proclaiming the values for which they stand to wider society. In their work with central and local government and other organisations they affect policy and attitudes as well as practical decisions. In one way and another, through the services they provide, through their campaigns and fund raising, voluntary organisations affect the lives of almost every individual in this country. A voluntary organisation whose policies, practices and approach embody equal opportunities as a matter of course can have a powerful and wide-ranging influence.

The history of equal opportunities

The term equal opportunities had its beginnings in British legal history. After the two world wars, many people who had become disabled fighting for their country found it difficult to get employment when they came home. After much lobbying by ex-servicemen's and servicewomen's associations and others the Disabled Persons (Employment) Act was passed in 1944.

Nearly 20 years later, when it became clear (as a result of studies by the research organisation Political and Economic Planning (1966) and others) that black and ethnic minority communities in Britain were also experiencing widespread discrimination, the term equal opportunities was enthusiastically re-adopted by champions of racial equality. In 1965 the first Race Relations Act was passed to ensure that black and ethnic minorities had the same rights of access to housing and other public places and services as the white majority.

Unfortunately, neither the Disabled Persons (Employment) Act (amended in 1958) nor the Race Relations Act 1965 had much effect. Further legislation was passed in the 1970s as the extent and persistency of inequalities, particularly for black and ethnic minorities and for women, became clear (Political and Economic Planning 1967). This included the Equal Pay Act in 1970 (amended in 1983), and the Sex Discrimination Act in 1975 (amended in 1986). A new Race Relations Act, strengthened in all areas and extended to cover employment, was passed in 1976.

In 1980 a Labour majority came to power in the Greater London Council (GLC) which, at that time, was responsible for running many public services for the whole Greater London area. One of its major priorities was to take a lead in furthering equality for all oppressed groups, and to combat aggressively the glaring inequalities in access to employment and other public services which continued despite the legislation. The GLC required all voluntary and other organisations which applied to it for funding to have an equal opportunities policy. Any organisation that wanted to benefit from the lower prices of supplies from the GLC also had to have an equal opportunities policy.

As a result of these and other powerful but often controversial measures, the GLC achieved a major change in the climate surrounding equal opportunities. Other Labour-led local authorities adopted similar policies. A number of private and public sector employers became, at least on paper, equal opportunities employers. Within less than a decade the idea of equal opportunities changed from a sleepy ideological abstraction to a controversial and high-profile fact of life.

This history and its political and emotional legacies are important in understanding equal opportunities and its significance for the voluntary sector, as well as people's attitudes towards equal opportunities. Many people have still not disentangled equal opportunities from its specific political history. They are ambivalent and confused about what equal opportunities really means for organisations. Many people associate equal opportunities with political extremism and with what they often perceive as the unfairness and even malice of the hard left. This is especially true for those who do not identify with the radical left-wing Labour image of the GLC.

There are other reasons why, after a further decade of active policy development and attempts to integrate equal opportunities into the voluntary sector, many people of good will are either ambivalent or disillusioned about the benefits of equal opportunities. For many organisations, the attempt to implement an equal opportunities policy has involved major conflicts and difficulties, and has swallowed up large amounts of resources without producing demonstrable benefits. Why then does the issue of equal opportunities not simply lie down and die? Why is it still in the forefront of debate and concern in the voluntary sector? Why do voluntary organisations still struggle with equal opportunities programmes? Why is there still such demand for equal opportunities training?

Despite recent history and experience, most people still feel that, at a fundamental level, equal opportunities is one of the crucial principles of the voluntary sector. The voluntary sector is built on the foundation stones of fairness, justice, accessibility and accountability. Equal opportunities is part of these; unequal opportunities is certainly not. This commitment to fairness and justice has helped many people stick with equal opportunities despite real problems caused largely by the way it has been handled.

What is equal opportunities?

Equal opportunities means ensuring that an organisation's policies and practices do not result in any individual or group receiving less favourable treatment on grounds that are not material; namely, race, colour, ethnic or national origin, creed, gender, marital status, religious belief, class, disability or sexuality.

For every organisation, moving to equal opportunities requires an initial vigorous and targeted programme of formal action. This must be based on a clear equal opportunities policy which covers every aspect and level of the organisation. The programme should enable equal opportunities to become part of the everyday culture and practices of the organisation and eventually be taken for granted. The results should be seen in terms of the way the organisation works at all levels, the way it recruits and manages staff and volunteers, the services it provides, the people to whom it provides them, its campaigning activities and so on. Equal opportunities helps ensure that an organisation fulfils its mission and is able to meet the changing demands of the environment in which it functions.

Equal opportunities in terms of meeting legal requirements

The aim of equality legislation is that all should have equal opportunities in employment and the provision of services. All organisations, including voluntary organisations, and all those individuals working within them, are bound by the legislation in Figure 2. There are also certain statutory regulations within the legislation which all organisations providing services must observe.

Equal opportunities as a formal programme of action

In order to ensure that it meets its legal obligations with regard to equal opportunities, an organisation must develop and implement a clear equal opportunities policy. With regard to employment, there are two codes of practice on equal opportunities published by the Commission for Racial Equality (CRE 1984) and the Equal Opportunities Commission (EOC 1985). These also require organisations to translate their legal obligations into formal policies with implementable programmes. The codes of practice are not legally binding. However, if an organisation has failed to comply with the recommendations and guidance they contain, this may be used as evidence at an industrial tribunal. There is also a code of practice on the employment of people with disabilities published by the (now defunct) Manpower Services Commission (1984).

A formal programme of action must be based, first of all, on a clear equal opportunities policy statement. Unless the policy upon which the programme is based is clear and explicit, the programme will lack clarity and direction. The policy statement should also contain a set of objectives setting out what the policy aims to achieve.

Figure 1 Equal Opportunities: myths and facts

What some people say.....

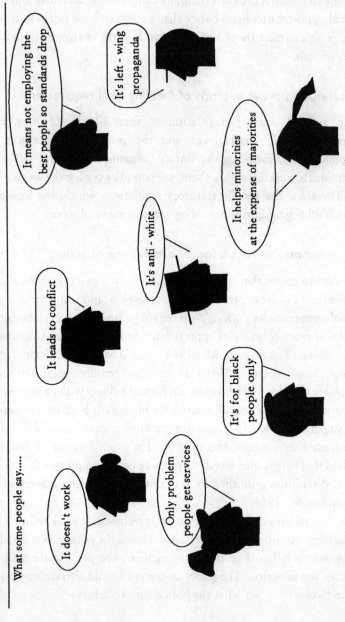

It's left - wing propaganda

It means not employing the best people so standards drop

It helps minorities at the expense of majorities

It's anti - white

It leads to conflict

It's for black people only

It doesn't work

Only problem people get services

Source: *Lambeth MENCAP*

Figure 2 Equal Opportunities Legislation in the UK

Disabled Persons (Employment) Acts 1944 and 1958

Chronically Sick and Disabled Persons Act 1970 (Amendment 1976)

Rehabilitation of Offenders Act 1974 (Exemptions) Order
(Amendment) Order 1986

Sex Discrimination Act 1975 (Amendment 1986)

Equal Pay Act 1970 and Equal Pay Amendment Regulations 1983

Race Relations Act 1976 (Replaced the 1965 Act)

Fair Employment Protection Act, Northern Ireland 1976 (Amended 1989)
1989)

Employment Protection Act and Employment Protection (Consolidation)
Act 1978, and its Amendments

There must also be:

- detailed codes of practice or guidelines to enable the objectives
  to be translated into action;

- a two to three year implementation programme setting out the
  steps the organisation will take to meet the objectives; and

- a monitoring programme to evaluate the effectiveness of each
  step and take regular stock of progress. This will enable the
  implementation programme to be reviewed and modified. (See
  chapter 4 for more about developing an equal opportunities
  policy statement and codes of practice, an implementation
  programme and so on.)

At the same time it is important to ensure that the reasons for the equal
opportunities programme, and its implications for staff, volunteers and
members are widely understood. Communication, through meetings,
courses, training sessions, conferences and so on—whatever is most
effective within the particular organisation—is absolutely crucial to the
successful implementation of equal opportunities.

Equal opportunities as a core value of the organisation

The idea of equal opportunities stems from the discrimination experienced by many groups who are denied their basic civil rights. The very existence of the idea testifies to the reality of discrimination. If discrimination, especially institutional discrimination,[1] did not exist, differences between people would simply be differences, to be taken into account, accepted and celebrated. But where there is discrimination, differences become a tool for stratification—a means of keeping people up or down depending on the group they belong to. Those features that signal the differences between people—physical differences, differences in speech, differences in style and manner—become the signs which distinguish those who are 'acceptable' from those who are not, those who can gain employment and promotion, benefit from services, and achieve representation, from those who cannot. The idea of equal opportunities, when put into practice, breaks the destructive cycle of discrimination, rectifying the effects of long-standing discrimination in employment and service provision, and pulling groups out from its cumulative effects.

Every organisation has an ideological base, a set of core values, though these are not always made explicit. An organisation's core values are important in shaping, for example, the way it is managed, the way decisions are made within it, the way staff, volunteers and members are treated, the extent to which people within the organisation feel accountable to those outside it, the attention they pay to organisational policies, and so on. To have any real effect, therefore, equal opportunities must become an integral part of the organisation's core values.

Voluntary organisations, founded on the principles of social justice, need to embrace the specific principle of equal opportunities. They need both to affirm that everyone is entitled to the same life chances and opportunities, and to accept the reality and richness of differences between people. Once equal opportunities is an integral part of the core values that drive the organisation, it will find expression in everything the organisation does. It will become part of the organisation's implicit contract with the community within which it works.

The principle of equal opportunities, when put into practice, also ensures that an organisation is truly achieving its mission, its objectives. Efficiency and ethics then become one, resulting in a more effective organisation whose practices, achievements, values and image form a single coherent whole. This is the ideal of most voluntary organisations.

Equal opportunities as a way of doing things

No two organisations are the same. However, certain indicators are particularly important in enabling people to recognise whether the practices of their organisation are based on the principle of equality, and whether it can claim, with integrity, to be an equal opportunities organisation. These indicators include:

- services that are accessible and sensitive to the needs of clients and members

- fair and effective employment practices

- proper representation in terms of staff, management, members and volunteers

- commitment to the development and empowerment of client groups

- overall concern with social justice and other ethical issues within the organisation.

Services that are accessible and sensitive to the needs of clients and members

An organisation whose practices are based on the principle of equality:

- provides appropriate and effective services to all potential client and member groups within the limits of its mission;

- monitors to ensure that all services are available to different types of clients or members, including those not traditionally served by the organisation, and decides ways to improve services where necessary;

- sees how the culture of the organisation affects the degree to which services are accessible and acceptable to different groups of clients or members, traditional and non-traditional, and makes changes accordingly;

- when making strategic plans, assesses and takes into account all the external factors that create pressure on and expectations of the organisation, even though this may challenge the established way of doing things; and

- is aware of the relationships between, for example, staff and members, staff and volunteers, and volunteers and clients, and of the image the organisation presents to clients or members and to the public at large, and makes changes accordingly.

Fair and effective employment practices
In an organisation whose practices are based on the principle of equality, managers:

- carry out fair and effective staff recruitment from the widest possible pool of talent and select the best candidate, without personal bias;

- create an environment where all talents, even those that do not initially fit the established way of doing things, are used to the full to make the organisation more effective;

- understand the support needs of different groups of staff and how to develop them to meet agreed performance targets;

- are aware of different work patterns and choices among existing and potential staff and help the organisation bring needs and wishes of the staff and the organisation together;

- appraise staff effectively and without prejudice, and make good post-appraisal decisions;

- will be role models of a healthy way of relating to and

working with people of different races, genders, sexual orientations and so on; and

- facilitate assertive and constructive communication about personal, departmental and organisational objectives.

Proper representation in terms of staff, management, members and volunteers
An organisation whose practices are based on the principle of equality:

- has a managing body which includes members from the various client groups and communities the organisation exists to serve;

- has a workforce and management that at all levels reflect the different groups in society;

- has a clear mechanism for monitoring the profiles of staff and members or volunteers, and programmes for taking remedial action as necessary; and

- has an induction and training programme for all volunteers and staff to explain the crucial role of equality within the organisation, and to ensure that they are prepared to support and work with it.

Commitment to the development and empowerment of client groups
An organisation whose practices are based on the principle of equality:

- has a wide and inclusive definition of its target client groups and communities within the limits of its mission;

- is committed to a continuous process of finding out how each client group or community views its own needs, strengths, potential and development, and the most appropriate ways of working with each;

- expects and helps its staff and volunteers to have a good understanding of the different needs of the various communities with which the organisation works;

- develops appropriate ways for each community of helping increase self-determination; and

- knows how to use, develop and renew the resources of the different communities with which it works, and encourages the ploughing back of resources, both financial and human, into the community.

Overall concern with social justice and other ethical issues within the organisation
An organisation whose practices are based on the principle of equality:

- has a creative and committed workforce that is comfortable with, and supportive of, the organisation's values and goals;

- treats people with respect and attention to their needs, whether they are employees, clients, members or volunteers; and

- presents a strong and confident public image.

Equal opportunities as part of the culture of the organisation

The culture of an organisation, though invisible, determines the way it works and what will succeed or fail within it. An organisation's culture is its 'atmosphere', 'the way we do things round here', the behaviour and attitudes that are accepted within it. The final goal of an organisation working towards equal opportunities must therefore be to change its culture to one in which equal opportunities is firmly rooted and taken for granted. This will ensure that equal opportunities is permanently and completely integrated into everything it does.

Recent research (Kanter 1983; Waterman 1987; Peters 1987, 1992) on the survival of organisations in difficult times indicates that those organisations that survive best have a culture that is outward-looking, flexible, innovative, accepts diversity, supports creative thinking and questions traditional ways of doing things. No voluntary organisation today can afford to maintain the opposite 'exclusive' culture which views the world narrowly in terms of stereotypes, and excludes or marginalises non-traditional groups whether as staff, clients, volunteers or members.

Organisational development

Why have all the efforts and resources poured into equal opportunities up to now achieved so little? Mainly, in our view, because the implementation of equal opportunities has rarely been approached as a piece of major change requiring careful and systematic planning and execution. More often it has been approached as a moral and political battle which has divided people into 'goodies' and 'baddies'. Major change of any kind, however desirable, is always difficult, and always meets resistance. Certain conditions must be met if the change is to be successful and lasting. Detailed analysis of attempts to implement equal opportunities in a wide range of voluntary and other organisations shows that these conditions have rarely been met.

Organisational development (OD) is one useful approach to the management of change. The discipline of OD draws on information from the behavioural sciences, including psychology, sociology and cultural anthropology, and aims to help organisations achieve lasting and fundamental positive change. OD has six key characteristics:

1 *A commitment to humanistic values*
OD is based on the principle that people matter and that the well-being of individuals within an organisation is important. People are also both more productive and more personally enriched in their work when they are given as much choice and responsibility as possible about what they do and how. In designing and implementing an equal opportunities policy, for example, wherever possible, the policy must not be imposed on employees but must be developed with their involvement and consent. This humanistic approach is particularly appropriate for the voluntary sector.

2 A balance between the needs of the individual and the organisation
OD recognises that there is often a tension between the needs of the individual and those of the organisation. A key OD principle is that the individual must not be sacrificed for collective gain. At the same time, the collective aims and performance of the organisation are recognised as equally important. Wherever possible the needs of both are met.

3 A whole-system approach

OD is concerned with the whole organisation; everyone within and connected with it, all its activities, the relationships of the different parts of the organisation with each other and of the parts with the whole, relationships with people outside such as client groups, funders and the media, external and internal pressures and so on. The OD approach is holistic, not fragmented.

The main focus of equal opportunities in voluntary organisations is on the delivery of services to clients and members and the carrying out of the organisation's other core activities, the recruitment and management of volunteers, and on employment practices. However, if equal opportunities is to become a lasting part of the culture of the organisation, it must also be carried through into other areas, for example, managerial style and values, the way the organisation monitors its achievements, and its relations with the outside world.

4 Change agents

In OD terms, anyone who triggers change in an organisation, who provides the inspiration, energy and means to carry it through, is a change agent. Change agents must build up alliances with those they are hoping to change. They need to develop their communication skills, their ability to collect data, their commitment and their integrity so that they embody the values they espouse. Their behaviour with each key group—clients, managers, staff, committee members, volunteers and funders—must reflect these values, as must every event and intervention in the change process. Although aggressive campaigning helps ensure that equal opportunities is firmly on the national political and legislative agenda, it is often counterproductive within an organisation.

People who have had bad experiences with the implementation of equal opportunities, who have been alienated by the hostility and labelling involved or the positions adopted, are often relieved to know that these are not necessary. Discrimination is unacceptable. On this there can be no compromise. But it is also a fundamental principle of OD that a change agent must have a relationship of mutual respect and open communication with *all* his or her colleagues.

5 Data collection as the basis of strategic planning

OD stresses the importance of collecting absolutely valid data about the issue or problem to be addressed and of then making that available to everyone involved. They all then discuss implications and so arrive at a shared plan for making the necessary changes. Many people collect data that are influenced by the results they wish or expect to find, or insist that their reading of the data they have collected is the only possible one. This creates polarisation and resistance and prevents development. OD uses the data collection process to create common ground on the basis of which an action plan can be successfully implemented.

The process of data collection, so often either ignored or carried out half-heartedly, is lengthy and time-consuming. But it is also an important intervention in itself, and, properly carried out, creates the foundations for a successful and lasting equal opportunities policy.

6 A self-help approach

OD is committed to increasing an organisation's own ability to help itself, so that it can rely on internal skills and leadership rather than external 'experts'. From the minute OD practitioners begin working with any organisation, they are also working out how to wean the organisation off themselves and make it stronger. This means identifying and developing the necessary skills within the organisation, and creating a situation in which people's involvement with equal opportunities will itself generate the energy to enable them to keep working on it.

Why use the OD approach?

The process of implementing an equal opportunities policy often highlights existing problems and ineffective ways of working within an organisation. Unless these too are addressed, those people who do not see themselves as benefiting from the new policy may be hostile to it and, at the very least, refuse to co-operate. Using the OD approach to implement equal opportunities is like taking an X-ray of the whole organisation. It helps organisations understand everything they do and how they do it, and so diagnose and remedy any problems they identify, creating a positive environment in which to plant the beginnings of equal opportunities.

The OD approach to equal opportunities is time-consuming and requires the active commitment of those people in the organisation who want to see the change happen, and especially of those in positions of influence and leadership. At the same time, it is clear that many of the approaches to equal opportunities that have been tried in the past— including borrowing an existing policy and bolting it on, making equal opportunities the responsibility of an individual or a small group within the organisation, and imposing it from above—have not only failed but have left conflict, disillusionment and anger in their wake.

For people—staff, management, volunteers and others—who are already overburdened and pressurised, the idea of lengthy period of diagnosis and planning and the commitment required may very reasonably seem too much. At the same time, we would argue that the successful implementation through OD of an equal opportunities policy will be of major benefit to their clients and members, to the organisation, and to them. And that the diagnostic and analytical skills that they will learn by going through an OD process will be useful to them in the future whenever they need to handle change. Such skills are becoming increasingly important in the voluntary sector.

Chapter 2
Who Should Take Charge of the Change Process?

Introduction

Faced with the formidable task of introducing and implementing equal opportunities, many wonder who should take charge of the whole process. Every successful piece of major change needs both a committed and capable change agent (see chapter 1) and the support of senior management. But research (Kanter 1983; Peters 1987, 1992) shows that the most effective way of achieving major and difficult change is also to set up a formally constituted team to take clear responsibility for it. Provided this team has clear terms of reference and a membership that is both credible and representative, its shared vision and its combined skills and energies make it very powerful. Representative membership—people from different levels, departments, occupational groups and political leanings within the organisation—pre-empts charges of bias and increases the team's credibility when conflicts arise. It also enables a wide range of views to be taken into account during the diagnostic and planning stages, and ensures greater accuracy and accountability.

The selection of the members of the equal opportunities team or task group[1] is vital. They will be largely responsible for the success or failure of equal opportunities within your organisation now and for years to come. Your decision about who should belong to the group, and whether to use an existing group or set up a new one, should be based on your knowledge of the measures that will be needed to achieve major change within your organisation, its culture, its normal decision-making processes and structures, and on the tasks involved in implementing an equal opportunities policy. These are discussed in chapters 3, 4 and 5.

Deciding the terms of reference of the task group

Very clear terms of reference will help ensure that the task group does a good job. Terms of reference are like a contract between the organisation and the members of the group. They should:

- state the purpose and goals of the group;

- outline the tasks it will carry out;

- state its precise role in relation to each task; and

- set out what will be expected of members in practical terms.

The role of the task group must be spelt out in relation to *each* of its tasks in order to avoid unnecessary and damaging conflict. For example, the task group will be responsible for drafting the policy, but will it also be responsible for deciding when and how the policy should be adopted? Or will it be responsible for advising senior management on this? Will the task group decide what steps the organisation should take to implement the policy? Or will it examine the options and recommend the best course of action to the board of trustees[2] to decide?

Details of the practical demands that will be made of members should include, for example, the number and length of meetings, how much 'homework' members will be expected to do, and how many preliminary briefing or training sessions they will need. It may also be necessary to state where meetings will be held, who will pay for any

Figure 3 Sample Terms of Reference for an Equal Opportunities Task Group

1 The group's main tasks are:

- to develop the organisation's internal equal opportunities policy on both service delivery and employment

- to identify the best way to implement the policy

- to set up group monitoring systems and schedules

2 The involvement of the group will include:

- drafting the equal opportunities policy and relevant codes of practice

- mapping out and managing the consultation process

- assessing the feedback on consultation and finalising the agreed policies and implementation

- holding discussion meetings with staff, unions and volunteers on issues relevant to the development of the equal opportunities policy

- evaluating the project

- giving feedback about how the project works to the board of trustees

3 The length of time needed to carry out the task will be up to six meetings (the first will last all day, the others will last two to three hours).

4 Travel expenses will be met by head office.

5 Managers' permission will be sought by the assistant director for members to join the group.

6 It is envisaged that the group will meet over a period of two and a half years until the tasks listed above are completed.

---

travel and subsistence and so on. If permission must be obtained from line managers for individuals to attend, it should be made clear who is responsible for getting that permission. Failing to clarify such things in advance can lead to conflict, both between group members, and between the group and the rest of the organisation. Figure 3 contains a sample set of terms of reference for an equal opportunities task group.

Exercise 1 Terms of Reference

Aims: To produce terms of reference for a group whose task is to develop, implement and evaluate an equal opportunities policy for your organisation.

Instructions: Write out clear detailed terms of reference for such a group. Figure 3 lists some points to consider.

Debriefing: Before finalising the group's terms of reference you need to consult with other interested parties as to whether they are realistic, clear and acceptable, and also whether they will enable the full implementation of genuine equal opportunities throughout the organisation.

Getting the group profile right

The abilities, strengths, representativeness and commitment of its members will be a major factor in whether the group is successful.

In terms of *tasks to be done*, you are looking for people who are willing and able to draw up one or more equal opportunities policy statements and codes of practice, to plan the implementation programmes necessary to achieve your organisation's equal opportunities objectives, and to set up a monitoring system to assess the success of the programme.

At least one member of the group needs to understand the practical tasks involved, to have a deep understanding of equal opportunities and its implications, and to have experience in tackling difficult equal opportunities issues. If there is no one within your organisation with this experience you may need to bring in someone from outside. This could be, for example, a colleague from a partner agency, an adviser from an umbrella organisation, or an external consultant. Before inviting such a person, check that they are happy with the group's terms of reference and can work with the organisational development approach to the process of equal opportunities change.

21

In terms of *managing the change process*, you are looking for people who are committed to integrating equality issues into the organisation, who have the interpersonal skills to work with, support and empower a diverse group of individuals, who will listen to and validate other views, and who can help lead the process of change through to a successful conclusion. You also need at least one positive resister (see chapter 3) who is committed to the organisation and its objectives but not convinced of the case for equal opportunities. He or she will provide useful information and insights for the group in planning the change process.

In terms of *representativeness and credibility* you need people who will be seen to represent different job groups and levels, and whose opinions and views will be respected. In particular, you need people who will be trusted and considered credible by those key groups within the organisation whom you most need to change (see Exercises 10 and 11 in chapter 3). If there is space, you may feel that it is also important to have representatives of client groups, funders or partnership projects.

In terms of *time and commitment*, you need people who can and will make available both the time and energy necessary for this task. Try and avoid a situation where some members consistently fail to deliver or drop out half-way through, unless their membership is essential to the credibility of the group.

The most efficient task groups usually have between four and eight members. However, it is also important to take the culture of your organisation into account. In some organisations it is necessary to involve representatives of a large number of groups and to have a task group of ten or more members. In others the group needs only two or three members. The decision on size should be based on your strategic aim of achieving maximum representativeness and ownership within the organisation, as well as on efficiency.

The following negative case study illustrates the importance of setting up clear membership criteria and terms of reference for an equal opportunities task group:

When a London-based charity embarked on developing its equal opportunities policy, it decided to set up an equal opportunities working party. Since race is a dominant issue for the organisation, they decided that most of the members of the working party must be black. At that time the only black people in the organisation were in administration. The working party was therefore set up with six black female secretaries, one white female policy worker, and the white male director. It had no clear terms of reference and no clear role or responsibilities, except to lead the organisation on equal opportunities issues.

The director neither delegated power to the working party nor took responsibility for introducing and supporting its initiatives through the normal decision-making structure which he headed. The working party drifted for a while until one member decided to capitalise on its lack of boundaries to achieve 'radical' change. Under her influence, the working party decided to enforce a requirement that each of the seven departments should submit an anti-racist monitoring report every six months. This led to uproar not, in most cases, because the white staff were not committed to racial equality, but because nothing within the organisation had ever been monitored, and the idea and practice of monitoring were completely alien. In addition, the culture of the organisation included very strong departmental autonomy; no department could hold other departments accountable. The demand to fill in compulsory monitoring reports on progress in anti-racist practice therefore pressed panic buttons within everyone except the members of the working party. The staff hit out defensively against the working party, and so began an extremely poisonous battle between black and white staff from which the organisation took nearly five years to recover.

There is no doubt that racism was an element in this conflict. However, much of the damage and suffering experienced by the organisation could have been avoided if a genuinely representative working party with clear terms of reference had been set up.

Exercise 2   Writing a Group Profile

Aim: To write a profile of the characteristics your equal opportunities group should have.

Instructions: Put together a clear profile for the task group, based on the criteria outlined above, and spelling out the skills, qualities, knowledge and other attributes they need to have. Bear in mind the strategic importance of the group in influencing the rest of the organisation and especially key groups in relation to equal opportunities.

Debriefing: Once you have drafted the profile, check it out to see if it is both realistic and genuinely representative. Try matching the people within your organisation—including members of staff, managers, members, council members, volunteers, clients and so on—against your draft profile.

Deciding on the right group

You should now feel able to take an informed decision on the best group to work on the policy in terms of both its profile and of fitting in with the culture of your organisation and the way initiatives are led. There may already be a suitable group in existence. For example, if your organisation is small and its policy decisions are usually made by a management team of three, this team, plus a staff and/or union representative, should probably take overall responsibility for the equal opportunities policy. If your organisation has an effective personnel subcommittee with both board of trustees' and senior management representatives, this may be your best choice, again with the addition of a staff and/or union representative. Some organisations use an effective joint consultative forum. Most often, a temporary equal opportunities task group is set up. This can be extremely effective, provided it is carefully planned.

Exercise 3 Deciding on the Right Group

Aim: To decide the best group to work on developing and implementing the equal opportunities policy in your organisation.

Instructions: List all the decision-making bodies within your organisation and consider whether any of them are suitable for developing and implementing the equal opportunities policy. If you think that there may be a suitable group, check its members against the profile you have written. Should anyone else be added to the existing group to improve its profile, or to make it as representative as possible?

Debriefing: Whatever forum and process you finally decide is most appropriate for developing and implementing the equal opportunities policy within your organisation, it is important to get agreement on your decision from the relevant management and other decision-making bodies. Otherwise, any work on equal opportunities can easily be marginalised and disregarded. If there is no suitable existing group, you will need to set one up. For more about this see the next section.

The issue of representativeness can cause confusion and difficulty, especially in organisations where there are few or no members of minority[3] groups, or where they are concentrated at junior levels in the organisation. It is important to think carefully about the role of any members of those groups specifically listed in your organisation's equal opportunities policy statement. They must not be marginalised, nor expected to achieve things that they are not in a position to deliver. A black member of the group, for example, should not be expected to represent the views of *all* black people. Nor should so much equal opportunities work be piled on the minority group members that they have no time to carry out their own work.

If you have no members of minority groups within your organisation, you may decide that it is necessary to bring in representatives from a client group or from another related organisation. It is important again to consider their role carefully, and to be very clear beforehand about the way you plan to work, your expectations of them, their expectations of you, and so on. Many damaging and negative experiences have resulted from unrealistic or unbalanced expectations of task group members who were also members of minority groups. They should be treated simply as fully participating members of the equal opportunities task group, recognising their unique contribution to planning the process of change.

Setting up the task group

There may be no existing group which, even if adapted, can carry out the important task of developing and implementing an equal opportunities policy. In this case you need to set up a special task group. Use the work you have done in this chapter to decide who should be in it.

The life of your new equal opportunities task group should be time-limited. Once the initial programme of tasks set out in its terms of reference have been achieved, its role should be reviewed to decide whether it should go on to work on the next set of tasks, or whether a new group should be formed, with new terms of reference and so on.

Exercise 4 Setting up a New Task Group: membership

Aim: To decide the membership of a new group set up specifically to develop and implement the equal opportunities policy.

Instructions: If you have decided to set up a new group, list everyone whom you might approach to be a member. Again, check the profile against that outlined above. Should anyone else be added to improve the profile of the group, or to make it as representative as possible?

Getting the group together

It can be difficult to invite people onto the equal opportunities task group without offending some and arousing suspicion in others. You can ask people to volunteer, or ask different groups to nominate representatives. The advantage of these methods is that they are visibly non-manipulative and genuinely democratic. The less the group appears to be a hand-picked group of extremists, wishy-washy compromisers or whatever, the better, though you can avoid this to some extent by making the group profile and terms of reference public, so that people can select themselves or others on suitable grounds.

If you end up with too many volunteers or nominees, use the group profile as a basis for de-selection, though with tact. If you end up with too few or with an imbalance of members, use the group profile to target the recruitment of people to fill the gaps. For example, if you have too many champions, recruit one or more positive resisters to allow objections and anxieties to be ventilated, ensure a proper debate of the issues, and prevent the task group from being seen simply as a one-sided 'fixing' group.

If your organisation has the type of culture in which most people normally accept and trust senior management decisions, it may be appropriate for the senior managers to select the members of the task group. Although this is less than ideal from an organisational development (OD) point of view, it may work better for your organisation.

Briefing and training the group

Once you have decided on the group that will take overall responsibility for the equal opportunities policy, you need to set up a briefing and training programme. The group needs a thorough understanding:

- of what equal opportunities is and why it is important to your organisation;

- of what is involved in introducing and implementing equal opportunities in an organisation;

- of the necessary ingredients of effective change; and

- of their practical and strategic role as a group and as individuals in the whole change process.

There are many ways of organising such a briefing and training programme while increasing the group's joint ownership of their task and help them become a genuine and effective learning team (see chapter 7). For example, you and the group could simply work together through all or most of the exercises in the rest of this book. Or you could invite other people from voluntary organisations working in the same field who have been through the equal opportunities process to share their experience and do some teaching, using the exercises as a framework. Or you could bring in an external OD consultant with experience in equal opportunities to work through the diagnostic and planning stages.

Chapter 3
Where Are You Starting From? Analysing Your Organisation

Looking at your organisation as a total system

Achieving change in an organisation means moving it from where it is to where you want it to be. In order to be sure that you are tackling the task as effectively as possible and changing the right things, you need to understand a good deal about the situation from which you are changing. You also need a clear goal. Only when you have information about *both* ends of the change process can you make informed choices about what to change, where to begin, whom you need to take with you, which approaches are likely to work.

Many of those organisations that have failed in their efforts to implement equal opportunities have done so because they have focused almost entirely on their goal. Organisational development (OD) stresses the crucial importance of understanding what you are changing before you start trying to change it. To do this you need information on three main areas:

● the problem to be addressed, in this case, equal opportunities;

Figure 4 Change

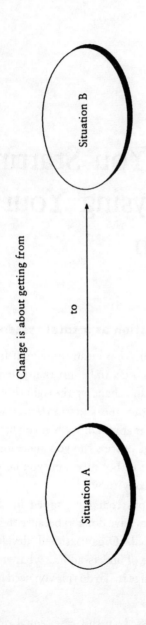

Situation A

to

Situation B

Change is about getting from

You need to know where you are now, as well as where you want to go, before you can plan how to get from A to B.

- the context in which the change will take place; and

- the views and perceptions of the key players, that is, of those who have an interest in the problem and/or have the power to facilitate or block the change.

This chapter provides a series of diagnostic exercises to help you put together information about these three areas to feed to, and discuss with, other key players in your organisation, and then to plan what must be done to achieve genuine equal opportunities.

An organisational model

All organisations, small or large, voluntary, public or private sector, have certain common, predictable features. These can be analysed and described in various ways or according to various models. (An organisational model is simply a way of analysing and seeing how organisations work. Different models emphasise different features, qualities or relationships.) The model most useful for our purpose here is adapted from the work of Nadler and Tushman (see Figure 5). It shows how the different parts of any organisation are linked and how the organisation itself sits in its environment. According to this model every organisation has six key interrelated parts. Major change, such as equal opportunities, affects all the parts of an organisation.

- **outputs**, what it actually does, related to its objectives or mission;

- **inputs**, including all the aspects of its external environment that affect it (for example, institutions, people, events, legislation), the resources available to it (for example, human, capital, technical, goodwill), and its public and private history. Inputs also include the organisation's strategy and the decisions it takes about how it should organise its resources in view of the demands, constraints and opportunities it faces.

- the **people** who work for it (whether as employees, volunteers or members), their knowledge, skills, needs, perceptions and so on;

- **tasks** to perform, what it does to convert its inputs into its outputs, related to its objectives or mission;

- **formal structures and systems**, including management and decision-making structures and processes, work processes, communication and information systems, monitoring schemes and so on, all set up to help the people in the organisation to perform its tasks; and

- **culture**, the informal arrangements of the organisation, the implicit unwritten arrangements and beliefs that influence much individual and organisational behaviour.

The characteristics of these parts will vary among organisations. No two have exactly the same mission statement or deliver exactly the same outputs. Similarly, the inputs always fall into similar categories, but the details vary tremendously.

This chapter contains 13 diagnostic exercises. Each focuses on an aspect of your organisation that is important in planning a major change. Where necessary, before each exercise there is an explanation of the thinking behind it and how it fits within the whole. At the end of most exercises there is a 'debriefing' section discussing the information you have gathered and possible conclusions.

Although you can work through the exercises on your own, we would strongly urge you to do them with a group of people, in particular, with the group who will take overall charge of the equal opportunities programme (see chapter 2). Working with one or more groups of people provides a wider and more representative range of inputs and views. Also, going through the exercises is, in OD terms, an intervention in itself, a step towards achieving your desired change. This intervention will be much more powerful if it enables a number of people to carry the momentum of the diagnostic process back into the everyday world of the organisation with them. Try to do all 13 exercises in one session in

Figure 5 A Model for Organisational Analysis

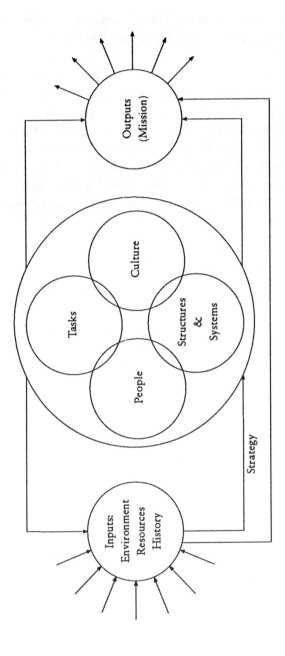

Source: Adapted from Nadler, D.A. and Tushman, M.L., 'A Diagnostic Model for Organization Behavior' in Hackman, J. et al (eds), Perspectives on Behavior in Organizations (1977). Reproduced with permission of McGraw-Hill.

order not to lose momentum. You will need to set aside a full day.

In addition to reading this chapter you may like to prepare for your diagnostic day by doing some preliminary thinking and data-collection, perhaps through interviews, observation, reading relevant documents or informal conversations with people inside and outside the organisation.

About half-way through the exercises you may feel confused, frustrated or be tempted to give up. This is a natural reaction, especially if this is your first full, systematic analysis of an organisation. It may be slower and more complicated than you had expected. Also, it may look as if the different pieces of information will never fit together to form an illuminating whole. Be patient. They will, if you can keep going to the end.

Exercise 5 Mapping your Environment

An organisation is an open system in which all the different elements interact with, and are affected by, the environment in which it operates. Different factors and forces in the environment have different impacts on the organisation and on different parts of it. For an organisation to operate effectively it must be aware of the often conflicting factors in its environment and must manage them strategically, while remaining true to its values and objectives. Changes in the environment also require a response from the organisation.

Aim: To identify all the external factors that affect your organisation.

Instructions: Draw Chart 1 on a large piece of paper. Write the name of your organisation in the middle. Around the circle list everything you can think of outside your organisation that makes demands on it, puts pressure on it, or creates expectations of it. Do not focus on equal opportunities in this exercise, but on *all* external demands, pressures and expectations. Do not worry if some of the items on your list overlap or seem to contradict each other, they often do.

Chart 1 Mapping Your Environment

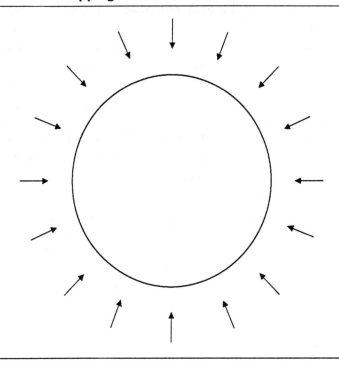

When you have run out of ideas, consider the question from the point of view of someone else in another part of the organisation. Keep doing this until you feel you have really thought of everything.

Debriefing: You may be surprised at the number of external factors that affect your organisation. Funding bodies and their policies, the different needs and expectations of different client groups, national and local government policies, the types of volunteers available, the local volunteer bureau, the labour market, UK and European legislation, competing organisations, public expectations, an ageing society, the diminishing pool of traditional volunteers, attitudes within society towards minority groups, the history and founding ethos of the organisation, the way the organisation has dealt with crises in the past, the views and wishes of members and social changes are just some of the possibilities. Some of these are obviously positive, showing the organisation where it should go or facilitating its work; others are negative, and hamper or block the organisation's ability to achieve its objectives; others are both. In some cases it may not yet be clear what they are.

You will use this list both in the next exercise and later, when you are feeding back the findings of your data-collection exercise to other people in the organisation.

Exercise 6 The External Case for Equal Opportunities

In Exercise 5 you listed all the external factors that affect your organisation and the way it operates. This exercise asks you to reflect on the arguments for equal opportunities in some or all of these factors. Here is an example taken from one voluntary organisation:

Among the many external factors that affect it, a cancer relief charity listed the following: the different needs and expectations of different groups of patients, a multi-racial, multi-cultural population, Cancer Research funding requirements, EU-initiated funding, health care and employment legislation, and competition from other charities. During the exercise to identify the arguments for equal opportunities in these factors, they concluded that implementing an equal opportunities policy would help them ensure that their services reached and met the needs of black and ethnic minority people with cancer, would improve their chances of getting funds, and would give them a better public image. They also concluded that they had to implement an equal opportunities policy in relation to employment in order to be sure that they were complying with employment legislation.

Chart 2 The External Case for Equal Opportunities

External factors – why our
organisation needs to take
equal opportunities seriously

Aim: To find the case for equal opportunities in the external factors that affect your organisation.

Instructions: Draw Chart 2 on a large piece of paper. Go through each of the external factors you listed in Exercise 5. For each, ask:

- Is equal opportunities relevant to this factor? If yes, how?

- Would an equal opportunities policy help our organisation deal better with this factor?

List on Chart 2 all those external factors to which equal opportunities is relevant. As you go, add any new factors relevant to equal opportunities and any new reasons for implementing an equal opportunities policy that occur to you.

Then review the whole chart and discuss whether and how equal opportunities is fundamental to the relationship between your organisation and the outside world. Make a note of the key points. You will use them later.

Debriefing: You should now be clear about the importance of equal opportunities in your organisation's relationship with the outside world, and about some of the objective reasons for implementing an equal opportunities policy. Once you can argue from a solid foundation that equal opportunities is fundamental to the effective functioning of your organisation, you should have less difficulty in carrying other people with you. It will be clear that this is not your personal hobby-horse but good organisational thinking.

Exercise 7 A Mission Statement

No voluntary organisation exists for its own sake. It exists to produce outputs; for example, sensitive services or an effective campaign, in a manner relevant and appropriate to its client community. All voluntary organisations should have a brief statement of what they exist to produce or deliver, often known as a mission statement.

A mission statement describes an organisation's essential priorities and values, answering the question 'What do we exist to do?'. 'We exist to provide intensive family support to disadvantaged families in inner cities' or 'We exist to campaign for decent housing for single homeless people and to influence central and local government policy' are possible answers. An organisation's mission statement is the touchstone against which all its present and future policies, programmes, achievements and requests for funds can be assessed. Should changes have to be made, it also provides a clear starting point for discussion. (Research in the private sector (Pearce and David 1987: 109) suggests that there is a link between a well-developed mission statement and good company performance.)

This exercise asks you to work out a mission statement for your organisation, in preparation for Exercise 8, in which you identify where equal opportunities fits into your mission. If your organisation already has a mission statement, and you are satisfied that it accurately states what it exists to do, you can skip this exercise and move straight on to Exercise 8. If your organisation has a mission statement but you feel it needs tightening, updating or amending, it is probably most useful to start from scratch and do this exercise.

Aim: To produce a mission statement for your organisation.

Instructions: Work out your organisation's formal mission statement, focusing on what it exists to do, or its intended output.

Debriefing: A voluntary organisation with a written mission statement which accurately sets out what the organisation exists to do, and which is known by everybody, agreed, and used as a basis for policy and practice by everyone within it is a rare thing. Congratulations!

Too many voluntary organisations pay little attention to what their organisation is achieving, to its actual output, and focus mainly on the vast amount of time and effort everyone is putting in. If your organisation is or has been like this, now is the time to act. Lock people in a room until you are all completely sure what your organisation exists to do and why it deserves to receive public money.

Exercise 8 The Internal Case for Equal Opportunities

Aim: To identify the internal case for equal opportunities.

Instructions: Look at your organisation's mission statement. Ask yourselves where equal opportunities fits into it:

- In what ways is equal opportunities an integral part of our organisation's mission? List as many points as you can.

- If equal opportunities is not an integral part of our organisation's mission, how might it help us deliver our mission more effectively and efficiently? Be as specific as possible.

- How will our organisation benefit if it has an equal opportunities policy? What would it lose by not having one?

Debriefing: You should now have a clear statement of the specific links between equal opportunities and your organisation's mission. If you have not, you might as well give up on equal opportunities now. An equal opportunities policy can only be properly implemented when the rationale for it is rooted in the organisation's objectives.

However, we cannot conceive of a voluntary organisation that cannot find the case for equal opportunities in its mission statement. The objectives of most voluntary organisations are all about providing services to, acting as advocates for, campaigning with and for, and helping to develop and empower people in those communities and groups which experience disadvantage, lack of provision or have special needs. Looked at this way, equal opportunities is part of the essential spirit of the voluntary sector. Take the example of the cancer relief charity mentioned above.

Looking at their mission statement they asked themselves, 'Are we currently capable of delivering sensitive services to *everyone* who has cancer? Are our counselling and support services appropriate to older black people? To gay men and lesbians? To disabled people? Is our staff profile a comfortable one for all those groups of people who might want to use us?' and so on.

Examined in this way, it becomes clear that equal opportunities is always at the heart of providing effective, fair and high-quality outputs—in terms of the way that services and campaigns are designed and delivered, of how staff and volunteers are recruited and selected, how members are recruited, how the organisation is managed, how publicity and other material is targeted and produced, in fact of every aspect of the organisation's activities. From the point of view of quality of output and genuine value for money, equal opportunities ensures that the organisation delivers. (At this point you may decide to go back and amend your organisation's mission statement to reflect the importance of equal opportunities in its objectives.)

Now you can summarise the main reasons why your organisation should take equal opportunities seriously, using the data from the exercises you have done so far. These reasons form the main plank of your organisation's arguments for implementing equal opportunities. You will probably add to them as you go on.

Exercise 9 The Tasks Your Organisation Does

In the next chapter you will go through the process of developing codes of practice or guidelines to ensure that equal opportunities is implemented in all the tasks or activities of your organisation. In this exercise you analyse these tasks in detail, focusing on:

- tasks directly to do with carrying out your organisation's mission, for example, giving legal advice, running training for care workers, counselling for victims of crime; and

- tasks to do with supporting your organisation in carrying out its mission, for example, fundraising, personnel management, administration, internal training.

For each task, you also consider how it is generated, and what skills, knowledge and values it demands. All this information will help you work out where equal opportunities needs to be introduced and implemented. For example, how will equal opportunities affect the way legal advice services are designed, delivered and evaluated? How will equal opportunities affect the visual images your organisation uses for fundraising?

Aim: To map out all the tasks that people (staff and volunteers) in your organisation carry out in order to achieve its mission, and to identify how equal opportunities should be integrated into each.

Instructions: List the answers to these questions on a large piece of paper.

- What tasks do people in your organisation carry out to deliver its mission or to support the delivery of its mission?

- In the light of your organisation's mission, are there any additional tasks that should be carried out?

- For each of the tasks you have listed above, consider what skills, knowledge and values it demands of the people who carry it out.

- What is or should be the impact of equal opportunities on each of these tasks? How will equal opportunities change or affect

  - the objectives of the task?

  - the way it is carried out?

  - the skills, knowledge and values it demands?

  - the way it is evaluated?

Debriefing: You will use this list in chapter 4, when you develop equal opportunities codes of practice and guidelines to enable equal opportunities to be integrated into all the relevant tasks.

Exercise 10 Key People: readiness and influence

People are the most important feature of any organisation. Their co-operation and support are always essential to successful and lasting change. However, any attempt to change things within an organisation also causes resistance in some or all of those affected. Managing the people aspect of change is therefore very important.

In the next two exercises you look at the people involved in your organisation and analyse their position in relation to the implementation of the equal opportunities policy. You decide who the key groups and individuals are in relation to this specific piece of change, assess their readiness to implement the change, and consider how best to manage each group to maximise support and manage resistance.

You may feel uncomfortable about grouping and assessing people in this way, firstly because such assessments are inevitably subjective, and secondly because they involve evaluation of people's attitudes and behaviour. However, we are not asking you to make a total assessment of people or to judge their worth in any way. We are asking you to assess the responses of key people specifically in relation to the process of implementing equal opportunities. This is part of rational data-collection and strategic planning. It is, of course, important to handle your assessments and any documents you produce responsibly and confidentially.

Key groups and individuals are not always those in senior positions or those with formal power, especially in voluntary organisations. People 'lower down' in the organisation may not have much formal power, but, because they deal directly with the public for example, they may have a great deal of informal power to help or prevent the carrying through of the organisation's equal opportunities policy. They are key groups every bit as much as senior managers. *Anyone* working with the organisation who can affect whether equal opportunities succeeds is a key individual or part of a key group.

Aim: To identify key groups and individuals and where they stand in relation to equal opportunities.

Instructions: Draw Chart 3 on a large piece of paper.

- In the left-hand column list every group or individual (depending how specific you decide you need to be in each

Chart 3 Key People: readiness and influence

Key people or groups	Readiness			Influence		
	High	Medium	Low	High	Medium	Low

case) who will affect what happens when the equal opportunities policy is being designed and implemented. The chart can be as long as necessary.

- Fill in the 'Readiness' column. How ready, willing and committed is each group or individual to accept and implement the equal opportunities policy? Score each group or individual high, medium or low. Don't worry about being scientific, go with your feelings.

- Fill in the 'Influence' column. How much formal or informal power has each group or individual on your chart to make equal opportunities change themselves, and how much can they influence the ability of anyone else within the organisation to make equal opportunities changes? Again, score high, medium and low.

Debriefing: You should now have a good idea of the positions of the key groups and individuals and of how ready they are to work on equal opportunities. Figure 6 illustrates different ways in which people can respond to organisational change:

- Some are enthusiastic *champions* of the proposed change from day one.

- Others respond quickly to its positive aspects and become *early adopters.* In terms of equal opportunities, early adopters are generally in favour of equal opportunities and the changes involved, but are not yet ready to stand up and champion the change.

- The middle group consists of *followers*, people who tend, even if slowly, to follow the consensus culture of the organisation.

- Then come *resisters*, either positive or negative. Both types of resisters have specific, fundamental objections to the proposed changes. However, *positive resisters* are people who

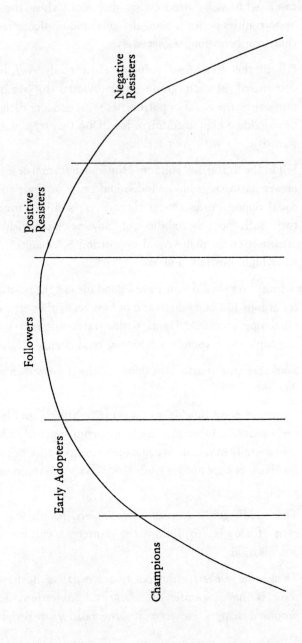

Figure 6 People and Change

have serious and genuine worries about the effects of implementing equal opportunities on the organisation or the way it is being handled, and feel they must resist the change. Their resistance can actually contribute to the development of the policy. *Negative resisters* are fundamentally opposed either to the idea and practice of equal opportunities, or to any change at all within the organisation, or sometimes even to the organisation itself. They try to block any change through passive resistance or sabotage, sometimes by diverting people's attention and energy into side issues, or by proposing such radical, unrealistic strategies that the organisation freezes and cannot face any change at all. Their resistance, if successful, will block change and will drain the energy out of the process.

Finally, there is another group of people not shown on the chart. This group consists of people who are genuinely not interested, possibly because they are coming to the end of their involvement with the organisation, or because they cannot be bothered with any upheaval.

We say more about how to deal with these groups after the next exercise.

Exercise 11 Key People and Equal Opportunities

Aim: To consider how to handle different key groups and individuals in relation to equal opportunities.

Instructions: Draw Chart 4 on a large piece of paper. Consider where, in terms of designing and implementing an equal opportunities policy and carrying through the changes involved, each of the key groups and individuals you have identified should go on the chart.

Debriefing: Each of the categories in your chart needs handling and managing differently in order to achieve the change you want.

Chart 4 Key People and Equal Opportunities

Champions	Possible early adopters	Positive resisters	Negative resisters

Champions If you have a lot of champions on your chart, you may be delighted. They are prepared to be identified with equal opportunities, to stand up for it unequivocally in discussion and confrontation, and to use their influence within the organisation to prioritise and support equal opportunities.

It has to be faced, however, that not all champions are an asset. Some are even a liability. These include champions of equal opportunities who indiscriminately shout 'discrimination!' whether or not discrimination has actually occurred, champions who as individuals or as part of a group are not respected within the organisation, or champions who take an all-or-nothing line on equal opportunities insisting on only one 'ideologically correct' position. Occasionally such people also use their advocacy of equal opportunities to increase their personal power by singling themselves out as ideologically pure. It may be unclear whether they are advancing themselves or equal opportunities within the organisation.

There must be no question of compromising on important points of principle in relation to equal opportunities. However, OD also stresses the need for sensitivity, empathy and flexibility in achieving successful and lasting change and in bringing people on board. It is important to be clear about where you can and cannot be flexible.

Inflexible and non-empathetic champions are a liability. You cannot afford to alienate or dismiss them, but you need to manage them effectively. It is important to try to help them see the need for sensitivity and empathy in managing change, and to take a realistic view of where the organisation is now and the energy and resources it has available for equal opportunities. Only then can you begin to use them to help you drive the policy through.

Early adopters You can dismantle the barriers between genuine champions and early adopters by setting up situations where the two can work together. The champions' commitment, energy and role-modelling is likely to pull early adopters into their camp.

Followers Followers have no strong leanings one way or the other, but tend to follow the critical mass of opinion within an organisation. Although their feelings are initially neutral, it is dangerous to ignore them in case they turn against equal opportunities. Their concerns over the design and implementation of the equal opportunities policy must be listened to and validated, and consensus found. Creating opportunities for followers to become early adopters will increase the positive force towards equal opportunities within the organisation.

Resisters If you have a lot of resisters on your list, you may feel discouraged. However, many positive resisters, once you have understood and responded to the logic of their resistance, will actually become highly committed champions. It is therefore important to distinguish between them and negative resisters, whose purpose, conscious or unconscious, is to prevent the implementation of equal opportunities.

Positive resisters are very valuable. Their objections and queries often remind change agents and champions of equal opportunities of issues which they must take into account if the changes are to succeed and last. They also have a part to play in ensuring that changes are not pushed through too fast or essential aspects of the process omitted. Within their own horizons, the work that positive resisters do is often of the highest quality, and their loyalty to the organisation and its aims intense. Your task is to understand the stance of positive resisters' reasons and to respond to them, helping them to widen their horizons and see the importance and the benefits of implementing equal opportunities.

For example, a woman who has spent years successfully organising white women volunteers may initially put up strong resistance to equal opportunities both because of the enormous impact it will have on her work, and because she feels that what she has done up to now is being rejected as worthless. OD stresses the importance of validating her past achievements and of making it clear *both* that you understand the difficulties and stresses that implementing equal opportunities in her work will cause, *and* that you regard it as very important that she should implement equal opportunities so that from now on, the service she provides will meet the needs of all potential users. Once such resisters, whose resistance springs from commitment and loyalty to the organisation and its aims, feel respected and properly validated, they often become vigorous champions.

Having understood the logic of a positive resister, there are always things about which you can agree. Focus initially on the well-being and good practice of the organisation. Respecting positive resisters and finding an area of consensus with them gets rid of the damaging split between 'us' (pro-equal opportunities) and 'them' (anti-equal opportunities) and creates a feeling of 'us-together' (everyone who cares about the organisation). When positive resisters are well managed, they can become super-champions.

Negative resisters Changing the attitudes of negative resisters is close to impossible, particularly since you would also need to change their motivation which is unpredictable and often difficult to ascertain. In addition, negative resisters are often defensive, especially if they secretly hold racist, sexist, homophobic or other prejudiced views. The most sensible thing to do with this group is to try to limit the damage they can do by out-flanking them. Try to make sure that they are not included in the formal change structure, for example, the task group, always predict their likely criticisms and accusations and work out sound counter-arguments in advance, and broadcast your counter-arguments widely through all communication networks so as to limit their credibility.

The uninterested Some people cannot be motivated to take any interest at all in equal opportunities or any other changes that will benefit the organisation. There is little or nothing you can do about this. Accept that they are not and do not want to be involved, treat them with respect, and otherwise ignore them. There is nothing else useful you can do.

The structure of your organisation

The internal structures and practices of an organisation are the way in which it organises and co-ordinates the task of converting its inputs—external factors, people, money, other resources and so on—into its outputs—the services it delivers, the other activities it carries out. Every organisation organises the conversion of inputs to outputs differently, through different structures, processes and practices. You now need to look at the internal structures and practices of your own organisation—how it is organised, how decisions are made, policies and practices communicated, co-ordinated and monitored—to decide how best to introduce and implement equal opportunities.

It is important to introduce equal opportunities in a way that fits in as far as possible with the way your organisation already works. Many attempts have failed because this did not happen. Some organisations even borrowed not only the content of their equal opportunities policy but also the way it was introduced and implemented, not realising that no two organisations can achieve change in the same way.

Analysing in detail how your organisation works may show you things you were not previously aware of. Good work and effective structures will show up and can be celebrated. You may also discover gaps, confusion and bad practice. This can be tough, but it does bring problems out into the light where they can be attended to. If the problems are very serious, you need to decide what action to take.

Bolting equal opportunities onto an organisation that is otherwise inefficient, unfair or chaotic is counterproductive, increasing the resistance of some peole to the changes and doing a disservice to the equality movement. If this is the case in your organisation, you may need to take the focus off pure equal opportunities for now.

You may have to go back to the beginning and sort out your organisation, working on, for example, aligning what the organisation does with its mission statement, creating fair policies for all staff and volunteers that make full use of people's talents, addressing problems in the organisation's culture and in the way work is co-ordinated and appraised, creating new lines of accountability and responsibility, sorting out clear decision-making processes and so on. Although this is a huge task, it is essential to the effectiveness and long-term survival of your organisation. It will also in the end ensure that equal opportunities is built in from the bottom up, since good organisational practices are also fair ones. You can use some of the exercises in this book to help people in your organisation see the need for change and to work out what needs to be done.

The organisation in six parts

In order to appreciate how the structure of your organisation affects the change process, you need first to consider some of the different possible structures that organisations can have. The are many models available for this purpose. The one we have chosen to use here is by Mintzberg, and is particularly useful in understanding voluntary sector organisations. Mintzberg, an organisational scientist, produced a model of the way organisations are structured, quite different from the usual flow chart of the organisational hierarchy (Mintzberg 1983). For our purposes we shall concentrate here on one aspect of his model; the organisation as made up of six separate parts.

Figure 7 shows Mintzberg's organisational model and how the six separate parts interact. As you read through the description that follows try to see how it fits your own organisation:

- The broad base of the structure is the *operating core*. Here are the people who deliver the core of the business; in a hospital, the medical, nursing and paramedical staff; in a medical charity that gives out funding money, the people who assess funding applications; in a family support charity, the social and community workers who work with families.

- The *strategic apex* at the top of the diagram represents the people who assess the strategic position and perspective of the organisation and decide which way it should go. In most voluntary organisations they include the senior management team, members of the executive committee, board of trustees.

53

Figure 7   Mintzberg's Six-part Organisation

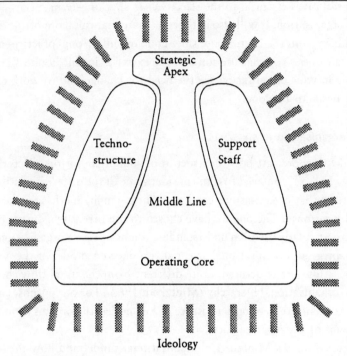

Ideology

Source: Mintzberg, 1983 (adapted by permission of Prentice-Hall, Inc., Englewood Cliffs, NJ)

- The people at the strategic apex hire middle managers to manage the people in the operating core. These make up the *middle line*. They relay decisions made at the strategic apex to the people in the operating core, and information from the operating core to the strategic apex.

- *Support staff* support the work of the people in the organisation. They include, personnel and human resource staff, administrators, finance people, public affairs staff and fund raisers.

- In most organisations there is also a *technostructure*. The people here set the standards of service or other output to be achieved, liaising with the strategic apex about policy implications and with the operating core about performance. In a charity bound by external legislation such as the Children Act, for example, the people in the technostructure monitor whether the service the charity provides is in line with the legislation, and liaise with the strategic apex about actual or possible policy implications. In voluntary organisations the people in the technostructure are often also middle managers and are very important in terms of making informed recommendations about and implementing equal opportunities changes or other initiatives.

- All these components always exist within an *ideology*, shown by the radiant lines in Figure 7. Voluntary organisations, in particular, always exist within a very powerful ideology, a commitment to a cause, which is the main source of their energy. For example, an organisation campaigning for people with Alzheimer's disease does so because it believes passionately that people with Alzheimer's disease have rights and that their needs should be met. This ideology, which is a vital part of the inputs of the organisation, affects all its systems and activities.

One of Mintzberg's crucial assertions from our point of view here is that people in different parts of the organisation usually perceive and react to things very differently because their roles, functions and responsibilities pull them in different directions. For example, support staff tend to collaborate with what is suggested and to help maintain change; the strategic apex tends to have a pull to control things from the centre; the response of the operating core, the people who actually deliver the work of the organisation, usually depends to some extent on whether the proposed change threatens or affirms their professional activities and identity; middle managers are pulled towards competitive ness and territorial behaviour, their response to proposed change usually depends on their assessment of what is going on in the rest of the organisation and whether going along with it will enhance their reputation; people in the technostructure always tend to try to move the organisation towards standardisation, and will generally accept change if it fits in with their pull to standardise processes, procedures, outputs and so on. In smaller organisations the conflicting pulls between different parts of the organisation may not always be obvious since one individual or group of individuals may perform several roles. For example, the director may also carry out the human resources function, set standards and monitor performance. In such organisations there is usually a pull between the strategic apex and the rest of the staff.

These group tendencies have nothing to do with the practical or ethical content of the change, or with 'goodies' and 'baddies'. They are simply a function of the roles, positions and responsibilities of different groups in an organisation. It is very important to be aware of them when introducing equal opportunities. Work out the pulls that are likely to affect the different groups in the organisation, and adjust your approach, emphasis and arguments for each accordingly.

Different types of organisations

Mintzberg describes five different types of organisations, outlined below. In each of these the six-part structure is configured differently. Again, each requires a different approach in terms of implementing equal opportunities. In Exercise 12 work out into which of the following your own organisation fits:

- The *simple structure*, with a small strategic apex and a large operating core that carries out all the other functions. The strategic apex and the operating core communicate directly with each other. There is no technostructure, no middle line and minimal support staff. Many relatively new charities, begun by a small group of people who both run the organisation and carry out all its functions, still have this simple structure.

- The *professional bureaucracy*, with a small, highly influential technostructure (often also the strategic apex) whose specialists monitor performance and promote the perfection of skills with a strong emphasis on training and specialisation. In the early days these specialists were in the operating core, but moved into the technostructure as the organisation grew. Most of the outputs are delivered by the pool of trained staff and volunteers in the operating core of the organisation. This structure is common among charities specialising in advice work and legal and social policies.

- The *missionary structure*, decentralised and enthusiastic, with a strong belief system at its heart which creates a pull to standardise the values of everyone in the organisation and all its component parts. Many self-help organisations based on shared life-experiences and problems have this kind of structure. The people in the centre depend on members out in the community with similar experiences and commitment to join the fight for their shared cause or to set up and run local self-help groups. In order to affiliate themselves with the parent organisation, local groups usually need to comply with certain conditions, though these are often vague and undefined.

- The *machine bureaucracy*, with a large strategic apex, and a separate large support function—including, for example, finance, public relations, fund raising, and marketing—which plays a major role in the organisation and mainly serves a large hierarchy of middle managers. Although the middle managers depend heavily on the support function they also often find it intrusive and irritating. Many older charities which have developed into fairly large bureaucracies have this structure.

- The *divisionalised structure*, in which a large parent organisation contains a number of subdivisions, each of which has their own technostructure and support functions and their own 'micro-culture'. This has occurred, for example, with many older charities which have taken on multiple issues with each division representing a different issue. Some of the international relief and development charities, for example, have a divisionalised structure.

Most organisations do not fit perfectly into any one of these categories but are hybrids.

Family Service Units (FSU), for example, works in close partnership with parents and children to prevent family breakdown. At the time when the intervention began, FSU had 23 locally-based unit teams, each with trained staff backed up by volunteers. It had a senior management team of eight, consisting of the director, four assistant directors, one finance officer, one training officer and a development officer. There were 296 other members of staff (full-time, part-time and sessional). FSU is governed by a national council of about 30 people who are its trustees. Members include one representative (normally the chair) of each unit's local management committee, the honorary officers of FSU (the chair, two vice-chairs and two honorary treasurers) and a number of independent members. The national council appoints some of its members onto the national executive council to oversee the day-to-day management of FSU.

In Mintzberg's terms, FSU is a hybrid of a professional bureaucracy and a divisionalised structure. There is a small strategic apex consisting of the senior management team, accountable to both the national council and the national executive council, and a minimal support structure consisting mainly of secretarial staff. The operating core is divided into 23 units, each with its own managers, so the 'middle line' is spread among the units rather than being based in the centre. The managers in the middle line, together with the senior management team, also

Figure 8 The Structure of Family Service Units

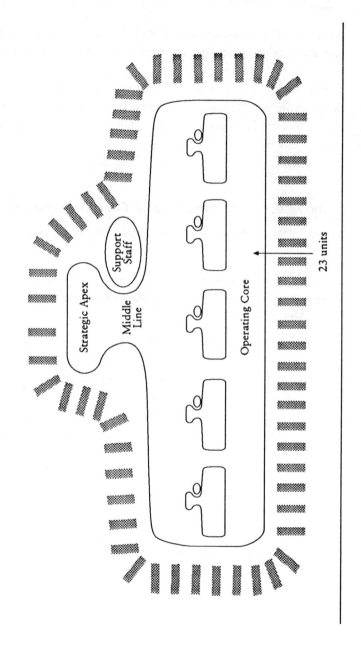

comprise the technostructure, maintaining the organisation's standards and the quality of its output. As Figure 8 shows, FSU has a flat structure, highly decentralised with few layers of management.

Any major change must clearly take account of the type of organisation involved and its internal structure. Equal opportunities cannot be introduced and implemented in the same way in a missionary structure as in a divisional structure.

Exercise 12 The Structure of Your Organisation

Aim: To understand the structure and type of your own organisation.

Instructions: As you do the following tasks, also note down any new insights or surprises you get from answering the questions or drawing the picture.

- Begin by looking at the numbers of people in your organisation. How large is your strategic apex? How many people carry out the core operations? How many support staff are there, and what do they do? Are there other people (the technostructure) who control standards and monitor the quality of your operations? How many? Finally, how many layers of management are there (the middle line) between the strategic apex and the operating core? How many people within each layer? What is the ratio of managers in the middle line to people in the operating core?

- Now try to draw a picture of your organisation, altering the proportions of Mintzberg's model and leaving out parts as necessary. Do not worry about the quality of the drawing, the aim is for you to have a mental picture of the structure of your organisation.

- Rereading the descriptions of the five types of organisations above, which do you think most fits your own organisation?

If you do not find a perfect fit, try constructing your own by combining features of the different types.

- When you have done all three tasks, consider how your findings should influence the way you introduce equal opportunities change in your organisation.

Debriefing: Here are two voluntary organisations described in Mintzberg's terms. As you read on you will learn more about the implications of different organisational structures for introducing change successfully.

G is a medium-sized membership-based self-help organisation in the health field. Its mission is to establish and support self-help groups throughout the UK and to provide support and advice for people with a degenerative illness. It has a small strategic apex (a director, two senior managers, and a board of trustees comprised of six elected members). The operating core is made up of a team of professional development officers and advisers. It has a large support staff who advise and inform the operating core, a very small middle line and almost no technostructure. In Mintzberg's terms G has a missionary structure.

M is a relatively new charity providing advice on housing for people with disabilities. It has a very small strategic apex, a large operating core made up of advice workers, and a very small support staff consisting of two secretaries and a research officer. In Mintzberg's terms this is a simple structure.

Now ask yourselves what you would do if you had to carry out a communications exercise with these two organisations on why they should take equal opportunities seriously. Whom would you involve? Whom would you leave out? What would you say to which group? How would the structure of each organisation affect all these decisions? You will use these insights in chapter 4 when you are planning the implementation of equal opportunities within your own organisation.

Exercise 13 How Your Organisation Co-ordinates Itself

This next exercise looks at how people in the various parts of an organisation co-ordinate their diverse roles and functions to deliver the outputs demanded by the organisation's mission statement. According to Mintzberg, there are five main ways in which they can co-ordinate themselves:

- *by direct supervision* in which, for example, A manages three people, and B, one of those three, manages another five. The major emphasis is on supervising individuals and teams to ensure that every one pulls in the same direction.

- *by standardising work processes* through detailed, clear, set procedures, often set down in writing. The focus is on how things are done rather than on the final outputs.

- *by standardising the final outputs*, setting clear targets and objectives, and leaving it up to people how they achieve them, providing they keep within the organisation's ideological framework.

- *by standardising the skills of the people doing the work*. If everyone has the same skills and understands each other's approach, their work and outputs will be co-ordinated.

- *by mutual adjustment*. This is the most common method of co-ordination in voluntary organisations where there is often little direct supervision or standardisation of processes. Outputs may be agreed, but people tend to function side-by-side as separate individuals, without necessarily co-ordinating or agreeing ways forward. Each person tolerates the others but believes they know their own job best. There is little accountability.

Aim: To identify the methods of co-ordination used in your organisation and assess their implications for the introduction of equal opportunities.

Instructions:

- Decide, with reference to Mintzberg's five methods of co-ordination, how your organisation co-ordinates itself. You are likely to find a mixture of methods, and different methods in different parts of the organisation. However, you will probably also find that one method is dominant.

- Discuss how effective the current methods of co-ordination are in helping the organisation achieve its objectives.

- Discuss the possible implications of the current methods of co-ordination for the way equal opportunities should be developed, implemented and maintained within your organisation.

Debriefing: An understanding of the main methods of co-ordination in your organisation helps you decide the most appropriate way to develop, implement and maintain equal opportunities. Each method requires a different approach.

- In areas where your organisation co-ordinates itself through direct supervision, you may decide to write equal opportunities practices into job descriptions and to monitor performance through the supervision and appraisal system.

- In areas where your organisation co-ordinates itself by standardising work processes, introduce equal opportunities codes of practice and procedures and monitor adherence to them.

- In areas where your organisation co-ordinates itself by standardising its final output, set equal opportunities targets and performance indicators for individuals and teams.

- In areas where your organisation co-ordinates itself by standardising skills, agree equal opportunities standards and ensure that everybody has or develops the necessary skills.

You will usually need a combination of all four of these

approaches, sometimes using several in one area. For example, in an organisation which provides sheltered housing for people with a history of mental health problems, it may be necessary to have a code of practice on interviewing clients, to write clear responsibilities into people's job descriptions and to monitor people's performance through the appraisal system, and to decide targets for providing services to clients who are, for example, members of minority groups or women.

If your organisation relies mainly on mutual adjustment, you need to work on improving its method of co-ordination *before* you introduce equal opportunities. It is risky to use the mutual adjustment method of co-ordination, with its continuous and often unsolved minor disagreements, conflicts and irritations and its general lack of pulling together, to implement and maintain equal opportunities. More formal and deliberate methods of co-ordination must be accepted and used widely within the organisation before equal opportunities can be successfully implemented and monitored. It is better to delay the introduction of equal opportunities until the organisation is ready to implement it properly and successfully, than to go ahead and fail, leaving a bitter legacy of failure, disappointment, suspicion and conflict.

Family Service Units (FSU), whose structure in terms of Mintzberg's model is described above as a hybrid of a professional bureaucracy and a divisionalised structure, uses at least three methods of co-ordination to ensure the quality of its outputs; direct supervision, standardising the skills of the people doing the work, and standardising the final output. FSU also has a Quaker history and ethos which emphasise co-ordination by mutual adjustment, manifested in people's relationships with each other and with the head office, and in the autonomy of the units.

Because of FSU's flat structure, direct supervision is provided mainly in the form of one-to-one support, and of mutual support within the unit teams. Standardisation of skills is necessary because FSU staff must be professionally qualified social and/or community workers, and must adhere closely to the relevant legislation. The output the organisation is aiming for is clear— support for families with the aim of preventing breakdown wherever possible.

All this had to be taken into account when planning the development, implementation and maintenance of equal opportunities within FSU. Although the senior managers (the strategic apex) drove and took overall responsibility for the changes, it was also very important to involve the unit representatives on the national council and the staff in all the units to ensure that they understood the changes and took responsibility for carrying them out successfully. This was done by, for example, devolving the training; putting some staff members through equal opportunities skills training and then getting them to train their own colleagues. This worked well in a flat, democratic organisation. However, the emphasis in FSU's culture on participation and on mutual adjustment as a co-ordinating method, and the autonomy of the units, posed problems in relation to the need for the centre to co-ordinate and monitor equal opportunities and to hold individuals accountable on equal opportunities issues. For example, the decision that no one could take part in recruitment and selection unless they had had equal opportunities recruitment and selection training, caused a good deal of conflict and anger. Although this was difficult, the people in charge of implementing equal opportunities had anticipated it during their preliminary analysis of the organisation and were able to handle it. (For more about the implementation of FSU's equal opportunities policy see chapter 5.)

If people understand clearly why an organisation needs to introduce equal opportunities, and have planned the process on the basis of a clear, detailed analysis of their organisation and the way it works, they are far better prepared to manage the journey, no matter how bumpy the road may become.

Organisational culture

Levels of change within organisations

There are five ascending levels of possible change within organisations:

- *Performance change* in people's own specific area of work. For example, people follow the laid-down procedures correctly in assessing a client's need for housing.

- *Work-based-behaviour change* in which people are able to transfer what they have learnt in one specific area to other areas of work. For example, not marginalising black and ethnic minority colleagues and listening to them in team meetings, or, in the general work situation, supporting colleagues who are being harassed, questioning automatically whether a new policy clashes with equal opportunities.

- *Affective change to do with the emotions.* Your aim here is that people should feel positive towards the equal opportunities changes and understand their benefits so that they will want to support and maintain them in the long term. It can happen that people feel positive towards equal opportunities and negative towards the process of change, especially if it was handled badly. This situation must be carefully addressed.

- *Genuine understanding* The first two levels of change are very much about following the letter of the change; 'if A happens, I must do B'. In this fourth level people grasp and embrace the spirit behind the change. Prescription becomes unnecessary. In fact it may be counter-productive, since dealing with equal opportunities well is complicated and needs creativity and flexibility. Once people have truly understood the spirit of equal opportunities they can take risks and try different approaches within the parameters of the laid-down policies and procedures.

- *Cultural change*, when the norms and values of the organisation have changed, and equal opportunities has become ineradicably rooted in the thinking and assumptions of everyone in the organisation. This is the level you are ultimately aiming for.

Change at one level can affect other levels. For example, cultural change allows and facilitates further progress towards affective change and genuine understanding.

What is organisational culture?

An organisation's culture is the commonly held, tacitly agreed values and assumptions that exist within it. It is the organisation's psyche. Even though it is rarely made explicit, culture is very powerful. It influences all organisational behaviour, dictates whether people are expected to be autonomous or team-players, to share information or guard it, to compete or co-operate.

Culture arises out of the organisation's history, growing from original motivations and decisions, and on layers of precedents. Even those people in an organisation who do not agree with its culture can still find themselves going along with much of it. A large organisation may also have several sub-cultures, evident in the different atmospheres in different departments—which jokes are considered funny, acceptable dress and language, how flexible people are about their roles and status or about time-keeping, and whether office doors are kept open or shut.

Working with the culture of your organisation

In introducing any major change it is very important to take the culture (or cultures) of the organisation into account and, as far as possible, to work with it. Otherwise, the change is unlikely to last, since the culture will not support it and may even work against it.

Occasionally, however, organisations have to go against aspects of their culture in order to deliver urgent equal opportunities objectives. In such cases, it is important to understand what you are doing, to plan carefully taking this into account, and to provide a very high level of support for people during this turbulent period.

Changing the culture of your organisation

Although it is important to work with the culture of your organisation wherever you can, this is not always possible. Because of their history, the cultures of almost all organisations are fundamentally discriminatory and unequal. Until recently, almost all organisations were started, managed and often used by people who were white, mostly male, middle-class, heterosexual and able-bodied. Inevitably the cultures of these organisations reflect the norms, values, assumptions, prejudices, habits and preferences of this group. It is therefore unlikely that you will be able completely to accept and work with all aspects of the culture of the organisation you wish to change. You need to stand up against and try to change those norms, structures or practices that are unfair or discriminatory, whether people are aware of them or not. In doing so, you need to be very clear *both* about what elements are not acceptable and must be addressed, *and* about your responsibility as a change agent to respect and work with the people you are hoping to change (see chapter 1). Providing that you recognise the inherent tension in this area, you can work out ways of dealing with it.

What kind of culture does your organisation have?

In order to achieve genuine and lasting change throughout your whole organisation you need to plan strategic ways to enable the change to affect and permeate its culture. The first step is to analyse that culture.

Charles Handy, in his analysis of culture within organisations (1991), identified four main types of culture, each of which he named after a Greek god:

Zeus

A Zeus culture is led by a charismatic authority figure who sits in the centre and radiates enthusiasms, passions and ideas. There is little emphasis on formal hierarchy and procedures but more on intimacy and intuitive mutual understanding. The closer people are to the person at the top the more influence they have. Because of the centralisation of power and the short lines of communication, Zeus organisations can respond to opportunities or crises immediately and intuitively. They work best with fewer than 20 people and in some ways feel very much like a club. Once the organisation gets larger, the informal, intuitive, leader-centred style no longer works so well. A Zeus organisation also depends very much on the quality of the Zeus figure and his or her inner circle.

The positive points of a Zeus culture include its informality and the fact that decisions can be made and implemented quickly. There are no cumbersome systems or bureaucracy, communication is speedy and empathetic rather than formal, and the atmosphere is often creative and exciting. The clear values that flow from the person at the top are shared by everyone. There is a high-level of mutual understanding and agreement. However, a Zeus culture can also be very exclusive and discriminatory. Only like-minded people are selected to join the club or get into the inner circle. There is also very little accountability.

Apollo
An Apollo culture is far more formal. It runs very much like a traditional organisational flow chart, with boxes containing job titles connected by lines showing management responsibilities. The organisation is seen as a logical machine in which each person has a set role to fulfil. There are formal systems, procedures and means of communication to ensure that the organisation runs smoothly and fulfils its objectives. Individuals are not generally expected to step outside their formal role or set of duties or to try to change them. Apollo organisations tend to be mature, and to assume predictability and certainty in the outside world. They find it difficult to respond quickly to the need for change or to cope with unusual circumstances or individuals. If something is not in the rule book, people often have to wait for the rule book to be rewritten before they can act.

Athene
An Athene culture is a problem-solving culture, where groups or teams

turn their creative talents and resources to different tasks. Expertise and commitment are what count, not age, job title, formal power, length of service or connections. There is little overt hierarchy, and the emphasis is on individual skills and abilities and participation rather than on formal roles or procedures. People are judged by their performance at a particular task, not by their adherence to their job description (if they have one).

Dionysus

A Dionysus culture is made up of individuals who want an organisation to provide the support and companionship they need in order to operate effectively, but do not want it to restrict or possess them. Often, the people involved are professionals who want to retain their identity and freedom. They do not accept direction from above, though they may accept co-ordination to further their own aims. Managers and managing tend to have a low status in a Dionysus culture.

It is unlikely that your organisation will fit exactly into any of the categories above. It is more likely to combine certain features of each. There may also be diffcrent cultures in different parts of the organisation, especially if it is geographically divided. You may, for example, have a Zeus head office, with regional units which are either Apollo or Athene, and a Dionysian specialist section. Whatever the pattern, understanding it and its implications for the way you approach equal opportunities is very important.

Exercise 14 Organisational Culture

Aim: To identify the culture of your organisation and consider its implications for the introduction of equal opportunities.

Instructions: Draw Chart 5 on a large piece of paper.

• Analyse the culture of your organisation in terms of Handy's four types. Is one type strongly dominant? Do different parts or units have different cultures? Fill in the first column of Chart 5. If you can think of another cultural type that better

Chart 5 Organisational Culture

Type of culture	Part of organisation similar to this	Implications for introducing equal opportunities policy	Managing these implications
Zeus			
Apollo			
Athene			
Dionysus			
Other (name?)			

fits the organisation, give it a name and put it in the box at the bottom of Chart 5.

● Discuss the implications of your conclusions for the way you should develop, implement and maintain equal opportunities within your organisation. Note your ideas in the second and third columns of the chart.

Debriefing: Equal opportunities can only be introduced into a Zeus culture if the person at the top is keen and involved. If you do get his or her support, the centralisation of power, short communication lines and intuitive mutual understanding and shared values of a Zeus culture should ensure that equal opportunities spreads quickly and soon becomes embedded within the organisation.

To introduce equal opportunities into an Apollo culture, it is important to take into account the formal processes of the organisation, to work out the arguments for equal opportunities within the organisation overall and within all the constituent parts, and to go systematically through the whole organisational map identifying each of the changes needed and how they will be formally implemented.

In an Athene organisation it is the people, not the systems, who are the most important part of the change process. The emphasis must be on highly participatory meetings and training, and on making it clear that good equal opportunities practice enhances the types of skills and talents that are so highly valued in this culture.

The Dionysus culture is difficult to influence. Since individuals in this culture like to shine brightly on their own account, change can only be achieved by providing opportunities for them to work out their own ideas on equal opportunities from first principles, and to discover for themselves the relevance and importance of equal opportunities to their work and organisation. Peer competition on equal opportunities with achievements publicised may help to engage people in the issues. Your main arguments should focus on the relevance of equal opportunities to their work, and on enhancing their professional standing.

Exercise 15 Your Equal Opportunities Vision

Most of the diagnostic work in this chapter has involved hard work and a heavy dose of realism. Now you need to take some time to dream. In this exercise you re-focus your equal opportunities vision to help you become absolutely clear about where you want to go.

Your equal opportunities vision is like the mission statement of your equal opportunities policy. It charts its direction, guides and fuels the processes of change, and is the touchstone against which all your equal opportunities programmes, actions and achievements can be assessed. It makes sense of and sets in context all the (often laborious) practical tasks involved in implementing the policy, such as writing and co-ordinating the codes of practice, developing an implementation plan, consulting staff and volunteers, revising partnership contracts, working with the management committee, organising training programmes, and setting up monitoring schemes.

Aim: To put together and refine your vision of what your organisation will be like when your equal opportunities policy is working and to see how your vision will affect your plans for achieving change.

Instructions:

- Draw Chart 6 on a large piece of paper. Discuss what you want your organisation to be like when the equal opportunities policy is fully implemented. How, in practical terms, will equal opportunities be demonstrated? How will people be able to tell that yours is an equal opportunities organisation? Think widely and creatively, focusing first on the outputs of your organisation, and then on its internal workings.

Chart 6   Your Equal Opportunities Vision

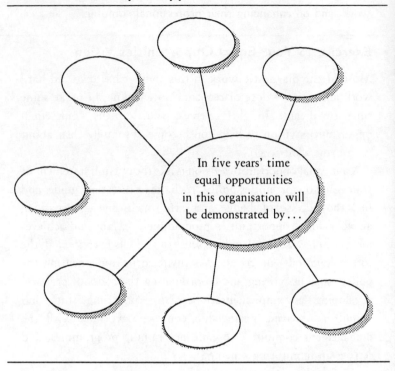

In five years' time equal opportunities in this organisation will be demonstrated by...

Write your answers in the bubbles in Chart 6. Be as specific as possible and add in a shorter time scale if you think it is reasonable. Add extra bubbles if you need them.

Discuss and note down your answers to the following questions:

- How do the vision statements on Chart 6 fit in with your organisation's overall mission? How will they make your organisation more effective?

- Thinking back to the diagnostic data you have gathered so far, how difficult do you think it will be to achieve each of these vision statements? How are people likely to react to them and to your vision as a whole? Will there be a lot of resistance?

Debriefing: Here are some examples from the list of vision statements of one voluntary organisation:

- In three years' time we will have representatives of all our client groups in all our decision-making forums.

- Our trustees will not only understand how equality is related to the trust's mission, but will actively support two or three equal opportunities initiatives.

- We will target two groups of jobs specifically at people who are hard-of-hearing and partially-sighted.

- All our middle managers will understand and practise equal opportunities management of multi-racial teams.

- In two years' time the proportion of women using our walk-in clinic will be 25 per cent.

- In two years' time we shall have a targeted project to provide more appropriate support for lesbian women.

Behind all these equal opportunities vision statements is the overall vision of an organisation that is truly achieving what it exists to do.

Add the information and insights from this exercise to the rest of your data on the organisation and on what will be involved in implementing equal opportunities. It will help you decide how best to move forward.

Exercise 16 Your Own Responses

Aim: To sharpen your understanding of what you have discovered in this chapter.

Instructions: Give each group member a copy of Chart 7. Ask each person to go through all the 11 exercises you have done in this chapter and summarise their own key learning points on the chart. You will use these in the next exercise.

Chart 7 Discoveries

Exercise	The most useful thing I discovered	The most surprising thing I discovered	I was most concerned by	I was most heartened by	The points I want to remember most clearly are
1					
2					
3					
4					
5					
6					
7					
8					
9					
10					
11					

Exercise 17 Reviewing the Whole System

You may feel that you have done quite enough. But you need to do one more exercise to tie up the work you have done in this chapter and make full use of all the time and effort you have given to it. If you stop now, much of your work will be wasted.

You now have enough information to enable you to look at your total system and put together a strategic plan for introducing and implementing equal opportunities. Look back at Nadler and Tushman's model in Figure 5. You should feel confident that you understand the model as a whole and that you understand a great deal about the way your organisation works.

Aim: To pull together and review everything you have learnt in this chapter in preparation for planning and implementing the equal opportunities change.

Instructions: Answer the following questions using the information you have gathered from the exercises in this chapter and from the chart that you have just completed in Exercise 16. Discuss your responses and put together a complete picture, including any apparently conflicting viewpoints. Other people's responses are extremely useful in gaining a deeper understanding of the complex nature of your organisation and of how to manage the change successfully.

- What external factors are pushing us to become an equal opportunities organisation? Which of these can we capitalise on to promote change? Which external factors create pressure against equal opportunities? How can we best manage these?

- How will being an equal opportunities organisation make us more effective in delivering our mission? How can we root the case for equal opportunities in our mission?

- What will our organisation be like when it is a genuine equal opportunities organisation?

77

- How will the equal opportunities changes be evident in our outputs, ie in what we do?

- How will the tasks we do be affected or changed by equal opportunities?

- Are the people working with the organisation (staff, volunteers, members) prepared to accept the equal opportunities changes? Do they understand the reasons for them? What resistance is there to them and what can we learn from this? How do we capitalise on support and deal with resistance?

- Are our staff, volunteers and members equipped to deal with the equal opportunities changes? Do they have the information, awareness and skills they need? What is their attitude to equal opportunities and to the changes? What must we provide for them in terms of training and other interventions?

- Do we need to introduce subtle changes in certain structures to help us implement and maintain the equal opportunities better?

- Do we need to change the way we co-ordinate ourselves? Introduce more effective ways of communicating? Of disseminating information? Of making decisions? Of supervising?

- What factors in our culture will facilitate the change? What will hinder it? What aspects of our culture need to be tackled? How can we do this?

- Overall, how difficult will it be to introduce equal opportunities changes into our organisation? Which pieces of the information we have gathered indicate that it will be difficult? Which that it will be easy?

Debriefing: Well done! You now have a thorough understanding of your organisation and how it works. The data you have collected will not only help you implement your equal opportunities policy effectively, but also help you manage and improve your organisation generally. Take a break! Celebrate! Feel very pleased with yourselves!

Feeding back the data to your organisation

When you have had your break, you need to consider how you will feed this data back within your organisation and to whom. This is an important intervention in OD terms enabling you to widen understanding and ownership of the change process and to use people's responses to help you plan your next steps. In times of change, more communication (providing it is purposeful) is better than less. The more the key players understand about the reasons for change, the better will be the quality of the planning of the change process.

The way you handle the feedback process and its timing should depend on what you plan to accomplish and whom you want to reach. You also need to decide who should be involved in feeding back the data and what your role should be during the feedback process. Your aim is to share the diagnosis in such a way as to gain the agreement of the key players. The data you have gathered so far will help you decide how best to do this and whether the task requires major intervention or something fairly simple and small scale.

For example, do you simply need to get permission to launch the project? It may be enough to give a written summary of your diagnostic findings so far to your senior management team. Alternatively, you may decide to work through chapters 4 and 5 first so that you can also give them a complete plan of action. Do you want to give your colleagues an opportunity to understand the organisation in which they work better and the implications for managing equal opportunities change? You could set up a workshop in which they work through most of the exercises in this chapter. Alternatively you and the equal opportunities task group could decide to wait and give them a complete diagnosis and a plan of action as well. Do you simply want to check with other people that the way you and the equal opportunities task group are approaching the change is correct and acceptable? You could set up a two-hour session for everybody at which you feed back your findings. Do you want to give people the diagnostic data and then engage them in working out the solutions to the problems you have identified? Half a day of structured exercises will give them the time to get involved and come up with clear solutions. There are many interesting ways of gaining greater commitment to equal opportunities as well as more information and ideas through the feedback process. Good luck!

Chapter 4
Developing the Equal Opportunities Policy and Codes of Practice

Introduction

In every organisation, the implementation of an equal opportunities policy must be based on a clear policy statement and on some form of written guidance, usually codes of practice or guidelines, covering, for example, operational areas, membership, the recruitment and management of volunteers, and employment practices for your organisation. This chapter sets out the steps you need to take to develop both and to plan how they will be turned into practice.

This part of the equal opportunities process is sometimes called the 'orderly' part. Although there is some flexibility in how the different steps are carried out and in the way they are handled, each one must build in an orderly manner on what has gone before. Without a policy statement, there is nothing on which to base your code of practice or set of guidelines. Without a code of practice or guidelines setting out exactly how equal opportunities should be put into practice in the day-to-day work of your organisation, you cannot work out what is needed to help people and the organisation to put equal opportunities into practice, nor require them to make the necessary changes. And unless you are clear about all these, it is pointless to think about monitoring anything.

The 'orderly' process described in this chapter is only part of the whole process of implementing an equal opportunities policy, discussed in chapter 5. It usually comes first, though you may also decide to embark on other equal opportunities initiatives at the same time, particularly if you know that your organisation is ready to change and that people are looking for signs of commitment and practical action on equal opportunities. For example, while its policy and codes of practice were being developed, one charity carried out a review of its past campaigns to see how well they had met the needs of different minority groups. On the other hand, if your analysis of your organisation's state of readiness has revealed a great deal of resistance to equal opportunities, you may not even be able to set up a group to work on the policy yet. You may need first to take steps to unfreeze the organisation (see chapter 5) by increasing understanding of equality issues among your key groups. You may be unable to find enough committed people to develop and oversee the equal opportunities policy until there is some positive pressure to counterbalance the resistance.

It is important to read this chapter and chapter 5 together, and to see them as describing two parts of a whole process. Once you have read them both you can decide where to begin, how to strengthen and support your organisation through the process, and at what stage your organisation should undertake the 'orderly' part of the process described here.

Summary of tasks

The initial tasks involved in developing and implementing an equal opportunities policy are set out as the first six steps in Figure 9. Usually they are all carried out by the equal opportunities task group or by people they appoint. Although these tasks take a good deal of time and effort, they are structured, and many people find them the easiest part of the journey towards a working equal opportunities policy.

Figure 9 Developing and Implementing an Equal Opportunities Policy

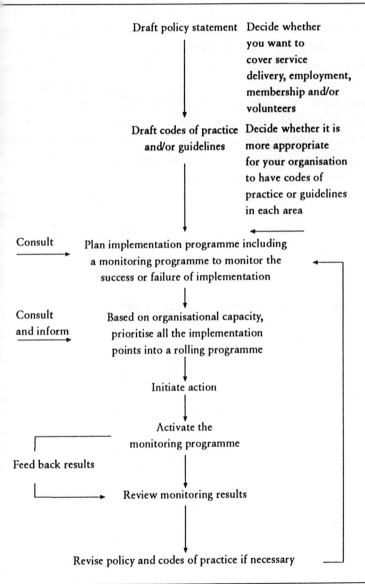

Draft policy statement Decide whether you want to cover service delivery, employment, membership and/or volunteers

Draft codes of practice and/or guidelines Decide whether it is more appropriate for your organisation to have codes of practice or guidelines in each area

Consult

Plan implementation programme including a monitoring programme to monitor the success or failure of implementation

Consult and inform

Based on organisational capacity, prioritise all the implementation points into a rolling programme

Initiate action

Activate the monitoring programme

Feed back results

Review monitoring results

Revise policy and codes of practice if necessary

Up to now, many voluntary organisations have tried to avoid the difficult and time-consuming process of developing their own policy by borrowing one from another organisation. In the 1980s, under pressure for contract compliance from many funders, voluntary organisations seeking funding often had quickly to become 'equal opportunities employers'. Many appointed someone to find out urgently who in their field had a good policy. Suitable policy statements were collected, sections pulled out, gaps filled, adaptations made, and the resulting policies produced for consultation. Other organisations simply adopted wholesale the sample policy statement supplied by their funding body. Often, however, this was as far as equal opportunities went. Very few organisations achieved genuine change or turned their stated intentions into reality. Although it is possible to learn from other people's hard work and to borrow good ideas on equal opportunities, it is an inescapable fact that a successful policy must be designed within and on the basis of its own organisation.

The equal opportunities policy statement

What is a policy statement?

A policy statement (sometimes called a declaration or statement of intent) sets out your organisation's policy on equal opportunities and commits it to certain standards and practices in key areas such as the delivery of services, campaigning, the recruitment of members, employment, and the recruitment, induction and use of volunteers. It states why the policy exists, and how the organisation will be affected when the policy is turned into action. The policy statement must be firmly rooted in your organisation's mission, making absolute sense in terms of what it exists to do, in order to generate the commitment and energy that are required to implement it.

There is no rigid rule about the structure and content of a policy statement. Some organisations have a single statement covering all their key areas of operation. Others have a separate policy statement for each area. In this book we follow this structure:

- a general policy statement for the whole organisation linked (usually) to its mission and setting out its objectives, followed by

- specific detailed policy statements (one for each key operational area) stating

  - the area this part of the policy covers;

  - (sometimes) the reasons for having a policy on this area, or the problems that the policy is intended to address; and

  - the objectives of this part of the policy, ie, how the organisation aims to deliver its equal opportunities vision in this area.

See Appendices 1 and 2 for two sample policy statements based on this structure.

Implementability is very important. The more specific the statement the easier it is to implement and to monitor its implementation. Compare the standard off-the-peg policy statement in Figure 10 (produced by one of the funding bodies) with the tailor-made statements in Appendices 1 and 2. Which of these would better help you implement a policy?

What should your policy statement cover?

Each organisation needs to identify for itself those major areas of its operation in which people require clear guidance to enable them to implement equal opportunities. We now consider what should go into the sections on these areas within the policy statement.

Outputs
This forms a very important part of your organisation's equality policy because it addresses the crucial issue of what it exists to do. It should answer the question, 'How will the outputs of this organisation be affected if the equal opportunities policy is implemented effectively?'.

Figure 10   Off-the-peg Equal Opportunities Policy Statement

Equal Opportunities Policy

.........Organisation is actively to committed to oppose racism, sexism and all forms of discrimination faced by minority ethnic people, by women, gay men and lesbians and by disabled people.

.........declares, therefore, that it will introduce measures that will combat all direct or indirect discrimination in its employment practices and in its provision of services and will campaign with those groups in the borough fighting to achieve these ends.

.........intends to ensure that equal opportunities in employment becomes a reality in practice and not simply a paper commitment .... will seek to implement a programme of positive action to make this policy fully effective by ensuring that no job applicant or employee receives less favourable treatment on the grounds of race, colour, nationality, ethnic or national origins, sex, marital status, sexual orientation, disability or age.

Look at the data from chapter 3 on the outputs your organisation aims to provide and the main tasks it carries out in doing so. Your statement needs to spell out why equal opportunities is important in relation to your organisation (linked to its mission statement) and what equal opportunities means in terms of its outputs. It should also say how you plan to turn your good intentions into reality. In addition, you may choose to set out the possibly discriminatory effects of the way services and other activities have been performed in the past or the problems the policy is intended to address. Here is an example:

The Goodacre Trust exists to fund research and development in the fields of health, social care and social policy. The trust's policy statement in relation to the funding of research on health begins with the current problem or shortfall, and goes on to say what the trust wishes to see happen instead:

'In seeking innovative projects to fund, the trust may unintentionally prevent access to minority groups because, for example, they may not fall within the traditional group of organisations who receive funding application information, or may not have traditional research experience.

'The trust is committed to ensuring that information about its funding programme is made more widely available in order to reach these groups. It is also committed to help smaller agencies to develop the necessary research and other skills to enable them to compete for funding on small-scale projects.'

The recruitment of members
You need to think about:

● why your organisation has members, what members do within the organisation, their responsibilities and rights, and how people can become members; and

● the total potential membership profile (national, regional, local, whichever is relevant), and your actual membership profile, considering how representative your existing membership is.

The statement should set out clear equal opportunities objectives linked to your organisation's mission, including enabling all potential members to benefit from your services, and covering publicity and the recruitment of members. It may acknowledge the possibly discriminatory way in which members have been recruited in the past. Proposals relating to the services your organisation provides to members should be covered in the section of the policy statement on outputs.

The recruitment, selection and management of volunteers
You need to think about:

● why your organisation has volunteers, what they do, their responsibilities and rights;

- the potential volunteer profile (national, regional, local, whichever is relevant for your organisation), and your actual volunteer profile, considering how representative your existing volunteers are;

- how people can become volunteers, recruitment, selection and induction processes; and

- how volunteers are used, managed and supported, what further training and development they receive.

The statement should cover the organisation's equal opportunities intentions on publicity, recruitment, selection, induction and other training, and the use, support and management of volunteers as appropriate. It may also acknowledge the possibly discriminatory way in which volunteers have been recruited, selected and managed in the past.

Employment

The section of the policy statement on employment should state why equal opportunities is relevant to the organisation's employment practice, linked to its mission statement. A genuine and effective equal opportunities policy widens the pool of potential recruits and ensures that the best candidates are chosen, taking into account all the needs of the organisation. Moreover, most voluntary organisations need a workforce that reflects and is equipped to deliver an accessible, quality service to all its client groups.

In this context, 'reflect' can mean different things at different times. Initially, it may mean that staff must be able to tune in to and understand the needs of all client groups. Later on, it may mean having a staff profile that reflects the demographic profile of client groups. It is worth noting that here, as so often, achieving genuine equal opportunities also increases the effectiveness of an organisation. A more representative staff profile will help improve the service the organisation is able to provide to its clients and ensure that its other outputs are effective.

The statement then needs to spell out the objectives of the equal opportunities policy in relation to all the organisation's employment and personnel procedures, including recruitment and selection, termination of employment, induction, staff development and training, consultation procedures, discipline and grievance procedures, harassment, promotion, conditions of service, the granting of fringe benefits, staff appraisal, job evaluation schemes. See Figure 11 for a sample beginning.

Figure 11 Sample Equal Opportunities Policy Statement on Employment

Statement of Equal Opportunities Policy

Save the Children is committed to the principle of equal opportunities. We aim to be an equal opportunities employer. Our employment policy aims to ensure that no job applicant or employee receives less favourable treatment on the grounds of colour, race, ethnic origin, creed, disability, sex, sexual orientation, or marital status.

SCF recognises that current opportunities in employment are not equal and that discrimination occurs on grounds of colour, race, ethnic origin, creed, disability, sex, sexual orientation, or marital status. It considers such forms of discrimination to be unacceptable, both in terms of good employment practice and in terms of social justice. It recognises that this situation will only change if specific measures are adopted to redress the consequences of past disadvantage and discrimination. It is committed to a programme of action to make this policy fully effective.

If your organisation has few or no formal employment procedures, you need to develop them first, incorporating equal opportunities as you go along. Although this may seem a horrendous task it will be time well spent. No organisation can be well run, or make the best use of its staff, unless it has clear and fair employment procedures. And it is bound to be counterproductive to impose a formal, structured equal opportunities policy and code of practice on employment if everything else to do with employment is ad hoc, unstructured, informal and haphazard. Introducing a policy that ensures fair treatment for only one or two groups within the organisation creates justifiable anger and resentment among the other groups.

Codes of practice and guidelines

The policy statement sets out *what* must be done. The codes of practice or guidelines set out *how* it will be done, and the support and resources that will be needed. To ensure the effective implementation of equal opportunities you may need several separate codes, covering all your key areas of work, for example, information giving, campaigning, employment and the use of volunteers.

The work involved in developing detailed codes of practice or guidelines on several areas of the organisation's operations can make the boldest heart sink. It emphasises the bureaucratic and policing aspects of equal opportunities, and reminds people, especially resisters, of its policing aspect. However, every organisation must take responsibility for making sure that its staff both can and do adhere to its policies. In many organisations this is well overdue. And it is possible to reduce the negative impact of documentation by ensuring that it is well written and presented.

Codes of practice or guidelines?

A code of practice sets out in detail what people must do and what practical steps they must take when undertaking a particular task. It is usually compulsory. Guidelines are more like a checklist of things that people should take into account. They are normally discretionary. Your knowledge of your organisation, its culture and the level of resistance among your key groups should help you decide which you need, or whether you need a combination of the two.

Some voluntary organisations operate entirely on guidelines. Others decide that in certain key areas of their operation there must be compulsion, with the threat of discipline if the code is not followed. For example, a housing association may lay down clear rules to be followed in specific areas of housing allocation. You need to decide whether such a radical step would be counterproductive at this stage. It may be necessary to wait until your organisation has been 'unfrozen' and is ready to accept some compulsion.

What should they contain?

The code of practice or guidelines forms a detailed working manual to show people what is expected of them. It should be as concise as possible. The main part is normally no more than ten pages long, with everything else attached as appendices. Some codes are only a single page long. All explanations, examples, forms to be filled in and so on should be collected in appendices at the back. It often helps to colour-code the different sections in the appendix for ease of reference. The language used should be clear and jargon-free with a user-friendly format, so that people understand exactly what is meant and do not find the document oppressive or hectoring. See Appendix 3 for an example of a code of practice with its accompanying policy statement. In general, a code of practice or guidelines should include the following:

A statement of the actions the organisation expects people to take and why
The reasons for the actions you are requiring people to take must be spelt out very clearly, especially if the actions are difficult or unfamiliar.

Staff in an advice agency were asked to submit quarterly records for the first time, indicating the ethnic group of each client. They were angry about the increased workload and concerned about issues of confidentiality. Managers recognised the staff's genuine dilemma over client confidentiality. They explained the importance for the agency of being sure that its services were benefiting all those groups who needed them and discussed the important issues of both client confidentiality and equal opportunities. Between them, the staff and the managers were able to come up with a solution that embraced both.

If you decide that your organisation is ready to accept some compulsion, it is important to distinguish clearly between items that are compulsory and those that are recommended. Anything that must be done for legal reasons or is a central plank of the organisation's policy should be compulsory. The consequences of failure to observe compulsory items in the code should be spelt out and linked to the organisation's discipline and grievance procedures.

Further definition of each action and a statement of the standards to be achieved in relation to each
The definitions and standards should be clear and specific, with detailed, realistic examples where necessary. Vague definitions cause uncertainty and confusion and make results difficult to monitor. For example, what does the term 'client record' mean in the example above? Is it a five-page prose summary, a set of scores on a diagnostic instrument, or a four-page itemised commentary?

Staff at the advice agency initially felt that it was not possible to find out a client's ethnic group over the telephone. After discussion and training they agreed that if they were polite and informative, people who would not normally agree to do so would probably give their ethnic group over the phone. They decided that it was reasonable to expect a 75 per cent response rate on this question.

A statement of who is expected to take the action
Some actions affect everyone within the organisation, others affect only specific groups or levels of staff. Avoid confusion and conflict by being clear about who is responsible for what.

Additional guidance for staff on how to do what is required of them

It is important not to ask people to do something new and possibly difficult or frightening unless you have also spelt out what they need to do and how to do it. You may also need to organise workshops and training for staff affected See 'Planning the implementation programme' below for more about this.

In a charity that relies heavily on income from its shops, which in turn rely completely on volunteer staff, the new equal opportunities code of practice stated that all recruitment of volunteers must be based on certain criteria. This was a bombshell, going against the values and strong beliefs of most of the volunteer organisers. The charity organised extensive training in which the reasons for the policy and code of practice were explained fully and people's worries and fears validated and discussed. Shop organisers were involved in reviewing the way they had recruited volunteers in the past and their current volunteer profile. They analysed the reasons why certain groups were not represented and discussed ways to address this, and the implications of the code of practice for the way they would manage the shops in future. Together, the organisers and the people in charge of the equal opportunities programme drafted an induction package for all new shop organisers which included equal opportunities. As a result of all this, the organisers owned and supported the code of practice, the induction package and the new way of working.

Drafting the documentation and carrying out the consultation

The most efficient approach is for one or two people from the equal opportunities task group to take responsibility (with help where necessary) for developing and drafting the policy statement, codes of practice, guidelines and anything else required. They need a good technical understanding of each operational area concerned, must understand the potential impact of equality issues in that area, and must be committed to equal opportunities. They also need close support, advice and critical insights from the rest of the group.

In some organisations, the senior staff on the task group carry out the drafting. This signals the importance of the equal opportunities programme to the rest of the organisation. Where the people appointed to draft the documentation need help in working out the practical implications of an equal opportunities policy it may be helpful to bring in someone from outside; possibly a colleague from a similar organisation that has already carried out this process, someone from the national or local Commission for Racial Equality or the Equal Opportunities Commision, or an external consultant. The stages in the drafting process are as follows:

- Decide which of the organisation's activities should be covered by a policy statement and by a code of practice or guidelines. Decide whether a code of practice or guidelines would be more appropriate in each case.

- Decide who should be responsible for drafting the policy statement, codes and guidelines and how this should be done.

- Decide how you will organise the consultation process.

- Draft the policy statement, codes, guidelines.

- Circulate copies for consultation to relevant groups and individuals, or to everyone in the organisation, depending on your earlier decision (see Figure 12 for a sample consultation form) and explain how the consultation process will be handled and what will be done with the responses.

- Comb through the responses to the consultation, deciding which comments to use and which not to. Revise all the documents.

- Produce a paper summarising the responses and indicating how they have been handled and why. Circulate this widely, including all key groups and individuals.

Figure 12 Sample Equal Opportunities Policy Statement Consultation Form

Team Members' Response Form
To be returned to   by

Paragraph	Comment	Proposed change

General comments

Signed   Date

- Once the policy statement, codes and guidelines are finalised, take them through the normal decision-making channels for approval.

The following case study illustrates the process of drawing up the necessary documentation for an equal opportunities policy:

Save the Children Fund (SCF) set up an equal opportunities task group consisting of the Director of Public Affairs, the Director of Administration and Personnel, the Director of UK Fieldwork, and an external consultant. Their job was to oversee the creation and implementation of the whole policy.

At an early stage, having analysed SCF's areas of operation, the group decided that they would require policy statements and codes of practice or guidelines on three separate areas of SCF's operations to ensure that equal opportunities was incorporated and integrated into everything it did:

- UK fieldwork, including guidelines on how to deliver a more sensitive and relevant service to children and their carers in all groups;

- public affairs and media presentation, including guidelines to help avoid creating a biased and negatively dependent view of the organisation's client groups in publicity; and

- employment, including codes of practice on recruitment, selection, training, development, induction, promotion and conditions of service. (For more about the development and implementation of SCF's equal opportunities programme see chapter 5.)

The group also decided that they did not have all the expertise needed to develop the detailed policy statements and other documentation. Each of the directors therefore set up and headed a subcommittee of people with the necessary expertise in their own area of work.

Once the policy statements, codes and guidelines had been drafted there was an extensive period of consultation with plenty of time for feedback. The equal opportunities task group and the members of the three subcommittees studied the feedback and responded to it, indicating which points they accepted and the corresponding changes to the codes, and explaining why they had not incorporated other points. The results of the whole consultation process were printed and copies made available to anyone who wanted one.

The length and thoroughness of the consultation process meant that most people in the organisation felt that their views had been heard and responded to. They liked the way the task group and subcommittees had handled the process and had held themselves accountable to the rest of the organisation. This made them more ready to accept and abide by the new codes when they were finally agreed and implemented.

Exercise 18 Drafting Your Policy Statement

This exercise sets out a programme for developing and drafting an equal opportunities policy statement. You may want to use the exercise (possibly with some adaptation) with the equal opportunities task group.

Aim: To draft a policy statement covering all your organisation's key areas of operation.

Instructions: Carry out the process outlined below to produce a policy statement which sets out your organisation's general equal opportunities policy as well as its specific policy in relation to each key area of operation. Use all the information you have put together so far about your organisation, what it does and how it works, its current practices in relation to equal opportunities, and your equal opportunities vision. You may need to bring in one or two extra people with relevant expertise to help you work on particular areas.

Try to keep the statement as short, specific, clear and precise as possible, checking it continually for implementability.

Overall purpose of the policy

List the overall reasons why your organisation wants an equal opportunities policy, related to your mission statement.

Outputs

- List all the key areas of your organisation in relation to its outputs (include relevant support functions such as fund raising and public affairs).

- (Optional) Spell out the current problems in relation to equal opportunities in each of these areas and/or why an equal opportunities policy is needed.

- Write the objectives of your equal opportunities policy for each area, specifying where necessary how you intend to remedy the existing problems.

Recruitment of members

- List the roles, activities, responsibilities and privileges of members within your organisation.

- (Optional) Spell out the current problems in relation to equal opportunities in terms of your membership profile, and of members' roles, activities, responsibilities, rights and privileges and/or why an equal opportunities policy is needed.

- Write the objectives of your equal opportunities policy in relation to your organisation's membership recruitment practices.

Employment

- List all the activities that come under the heading of employment practices in your organisation, including recruitment, selection and promotion, appraisal, dealing with harassment, induction, training and development and so on.

- (Optional) Spell out the current problems in relation to equal opportunities in terms of your employment practices and/or why an equal opportunities policy is needed.

- Write the objectives of your equal opportunities policy in relation to all the organisation's employment practices.

Volunteers

- List the roles, activities, responsibilities, rights and privileges of volunteers within your organisation.

- List the main areas of recruitment and management of volunteers (including publicity, selection, induction, deployment, support and so on).

- (Optional) Spell out the current problems in relation to equal opportunities in terms of your volunteer profile, of volunteers' roles, activities, responsibilities, rights and privileges, and of the way they are recruited and managed and/or why an equal opportunities policy is needed.

- Write the objectives of your equal opportunities policy in relation to your organisation's recruitment and management of volunteers.

Exercise 19 Drafting Your Codes of Practice and/or Guidelines

This exercise sets out a list of tasks for developing and drafting equal opportunities codes of practice and guidelines. You may want to use it (possibly with some adaptation) as part of the planning process with your equal opportunities task group.

Aim: To identify all the codes of practice and/or guidelines that are needed in order for your organisation's equal opportunities policy statement to be implemented, and to plan how a final version of each will be produced.

Instructions: Look at the policy statement you produced in the previous exercise. Which sections need to be backed up by further guidance, direction, or support to help people implement them?

In each case consider:

- Should the back-up be in the form of codes of practice or guidelines?

- What are the organisation's objectives in this area?

- What are the main problems that need to be addressed and the main changes that need to be made?

- Which are the main groups that will be affected by the code of practice or guidelines? How ready are they to accept and implement the changes involved? What support or development do they need?

- Are there any existing guidelines or codes of practice in this area? If yes, can equal opportunities issues be integrated into a revised version? If no, what else should be included in the new guidelines or codes of practice to make them more comprehensive?

- Who should be involved in the detailed drafting? Who should be consulted on the draft?

Once you have considered all these questions you have enough data to enable one or more selected individuals to draft and eventually finalise the codes of practice or guidelines.

- Make a list of what needs to be done to get the codes or guidelines drafted, finalised and circulated.

- Decide who will be responsible for each step and work out a timetable for action.

- Make sure that they fully understand their task(s), are clear about what they are aiming to produce, and know where to go for help and support should they need it.

Planning the implementation programme

If you have got this far, you have good cause for celebration. You have laid the groundwork for a major piece of development within your organisation, and have initiated a very important piece of cultural change. You are also streets ahead of most voluntary organisations.

However, you still have one more piece of hard orderly work before this part of the job is done. The aim of the codes of practice and guidelines is to enable individuals to take on the responsibility for making equal opportunities a normal part of the everyday operation of your organisation. This last piece of work involves the organisation taking responsibility for supporting, resourcing and enabling this to happen.

Exercise 20 Planning the Implementation Programme

The task of planning an implementation programme for each code of practice or set of guidelines should be done in each case by the main people who will be responsible for ensuring that the programme is carried out, under the overall direction and supervision of the equal opportunities task group.

Aim: To produce a detailed implementation programme for all the new codes of practice and guidelines.

Instructions: For each code of practice or guidelines:

- Comb systematically through the code or guidelines and work out in detail all the steps that must be taken to ensure that people can and do turn it into practice. For every item ask yourself 'What action is needed for people to turn this item from theory into practice?'.

- List the actions you identify. These may include, for example, additional or special resources, training or development, changes in the way they organise their work, additional support, or changed practices in other areas of the organisation.

- For each action, work out what resources will be required, in terms of people, time, money, facilities, equipment, documentation, negotiation.

- Decide who will have overall responsibility for making sure that each action is carried out.

- Decide a reasonable timescale, dividing your list of actions to be taken into long and short term.

- Pull out of your list all the relatively straightforward administrative tasks and delegate them to one or more members of the group.

- Pull out of your list any projects or major pieces of work requiring further planning and multiple co-operation such as, for example, a positive action training programme for women, or an audit of jobs in your organisation with regard to disability. Break them down into smaller chunks of work.

- Work out a reasonable rolling programme of projects and actions to be carried out over the next two or three years, using the following criteria to decide the order and timing:

  - urgency in meeting a particular need

  - achieving commitment to and creating credibility for the whole programme

  - likely levels of resistance or support

  - importance in terms of initiating the programme

  - importance in terms of the core objectives of the whole programme

- importance in terms of achieving public credibility.

- Weight the projects on your list in terms of urgency.

- Fill in your whole rolling programme with all the necessary details using charts similar to those in Figures 13 and 14.

Debriefing: The comprehensive rolling implementation programme you have worked out is likely to seem daunting. It is very important to break it up into workable chunks and not to sabotage the whole equal opportunities programme by overloading everyone. Encourage yourselves with the certain knowledge that the benefits to your organisation of this whole process will be tremendous, and not simply in terms of equal opportunities. Your organisation will begin to understand itself much better, and, after inevitable initial eruptions and difficulties, people's morale and the levels of trust and communication between them will improve. Problems in the way the organisation functions will become obvious and can be rectified.

The following case studies show how the process of planning the implementation programme was handled in two voluntary organisations:

Organisation B has the following clause in its new code of practice on the recruitment and use of volunteers: 'All volunteer organisers must from now on use a person profile in recruiting volunteers.'

The task group set up to oversee the implementation of Organisation B's equal opportunities policy came up with the following list of major actions to ensure the implementation of this clause, setting out who should do the work and, where possible, by when:

- Draft a person profile of volunteers for the organisation. Include all relevant characteristics, including volunteers'

Figure 13 Sample Implementation Programme Chart

Item in code of practice	Long-term action programme	Resources needed	Cost	Delegated to	Schedule

Figure 14 Sample Implementation Timetable

Jan	Feb	Mar	Apr	May	June	July	Aug	Sept	Oct	Nov	Dec

willingness to adhere to our equality policies and practices. (Joan, 2 weeks)

- Check that this profile can be applied equally to all volunteers, including those running the shop, helping in the office, collecting funds, and helping in the day-care centre. Test run the profile on several existing volunteers. (Joan in consultation with all volunteer organisers, 2 months)

- Decide how to use the profile with existing volunteers, and the training needed to ensure that they understand and are committed to the equal opportunities policy. (Training officers and Joan, for next year's training programme)

- Check the person profile against our traditional sources of volunteers. Decide whether we need to cultivate new sources, how this should be done and by whom. (Joan, Daljit and Grace, by Christmas)

- If it proves unrealistic to adhere strictly to the new profile in recruiting new volunteers, develop an induction programme for new volunteers to ensure that they understand and are committed to the equal opportunities policy. (Training officer and Joan)

- Set up a communication programme to ensure that everyone involved in recruiting, inducting, managing and training volunteers understands the new policy and code of practice and is able to work with it. (Joan, Daljit, Grace and training officer)

The group then went through the whole list again in detail and worked out how each step would be done and what resources would be needed. For the training of their 56 volunteer organisers, for example, they decided to set up four half-day training sessions. The training officer undertook to organise these, and a source of funds for expenses was identified.

When the group had combed right through the code of practice and listed all the tasks to be done and by whom, they felt overwhelmed. They decided to sort the list into urgent and less urgent tasks. They then worked out a rolling prioritised programme of action over the next two years which they felt they, the staff and volunteers, and the organisation could manage.

The Goodacre Trust's research department staff (see above) set up a meeting to discuss practical steps to implement their stated commitment. They produced this list:

To try to ensure equal access for all groups to health research grants we will:

- assess the way we circulate information about grants at present;

- carry out a short survey targeted at minority organisations to find out whether they know about our grant programme;

- monitor the types of organisations that submit funding applications;

- review our publicity material to see whether it gives a narrow picture of our client group and might put off other types of clients;

- on the basis of all this, redesign our dissemination strategy;

- allocate certain research topics to groups with particular expertise in these areas, including non-traditional organisations;

- run open days to give information to organisations who want to know more about us but are not part of our existing network;

- set up a secondment scheme for staff from under-represented organisations to work in our department and improve their research and other skills; and

- set up a positive action programme for trainees from under-represented groups such as refugees, black and ethnic minority groups, people with disabilities.

This list may look exhausting, but it is also clearly targeted and well thought out. Their final step was to prioritise the items, and to set up an implementable rolling programme.

Monitoring and evaluation

Once the implementation programme has begun, you need to begin to monitor how well it is working and to evaluate progress towards the full implementation of equal opportunities. Is all this hard work achieving anything?

Monitoring and evaluation are dealt with more fully in chapter 6. However, it is worth saying at this point that there there are four aspects of the programme which it is particularly useful to monitor. You need to consider how to do this while you are planning the implementation programme:

- Numerical data on the characteristics of employees, applicants, members, volunteers and so on. Such data enable you to find out which groups may be under-represented and in which areas, to develop a programme to remedy this situation, and to monitor its success.

- Organisational procedures such as selection, recruitment, appraisal, deployment of volunteers, to check for directly or indirectly discriminatory effects and decide what needs to be changed.

- Specific equal opportunities initiatives and projects, such as disability awareness training, or including equal opportunities duties on appraisal forms. Are these initiatives producing measurable results? If not, what do you need to change? Is the project worth continuing?

- Qualitative monitoring of the way people are working. For example, how effective managers are in implementing the equal opportunities policy, whether the recruitment panel is making better decisions. These areas are difficult to monitor but are, in some ways, the most important outcomes of the whole equal opportunities policy.

In each case, the more specific and clear the objectives and actions set out in your implementation programme, the easier it will be to find out if they are being achieved.

Chapter 5
Becoming an Equal Opportunities Organisation–the Next Steps

Introduction

You now have a lot of information about your organisation, the way it works, and the key people and groups working with it. You know where equal opportunities fits into your organisation's objectives, how it is likely to respond to the proposed equal opportunities changes, and who should take charge of the whole equal opportunities programme. You know what needs to be done to develop an implementable policy and codes of practice.

But developing and implementing the policy and codes of practice is only part of a wider change programme whose final objective is to make equal opportunities one of the core values which drives your organisation and to integrate it permanently into your organisational culture and activities. You now need to step back and look at your whole organisation, considering what other changes are needed to move it towards the equal opportunities vision which has been developed. At the end of this chapter is an exercise which sets out the questions you need to consider in producing a full and effective implementation plan.

Once again, the exercise and the thinking that precedes it are best done by a group of people, including your equal opportunities task force.

Many people at this point worry whether it will all work. However much data you have, you still cannot have total control over the process or be 100 per cent sure of the consequences of your decisions. Some of the key factors may change as you progress.

Although these worries are real, you need to keep them in check. Hold on to the knowledge that you have done all the spade work and that you are as well prepared as possible to begin making the changes. Although you may not get things 100 per cent right, you and your organisation are starting from a much surer foundation than those organisations that have leapt into introducing equal opportunities without any serious analysis at all. The systemic diagnosis and planning you have done will be your anchor and guide when unexpected factors assail your plan and threaten to push it off course.

How to decide what to do

Now that you have decided what you want to achieve and where you want to end up, you need to choose which of the wide range of possible interventions will best get you there. Remember that the best way for *your* organisation will be different from any other organisation's best way, since every organisation is different.

Is this the right intervention for this phase of change?

Once it has been decided to embark upon equal opportunities, there is often tremendous pressure to move fast and to be seen to change everything immediately. Those responsible for managing the changes may be accused of lacking commitment or of incompetence if they move slowly and deliberately. But any major change, especially one as complex as equal opportunities, takes a long time. Rushing in and doing everything at once inevitably means disregarding the culture and context of the organisation. It achieves short-term high-visibility change rather than genuine development, and is unlikely to last.

It is helpful to see change as occurring in three main 'phases':

- unfreezing

- moving

- refreezing or institutionalising (Lewin 1958; Lippitt, Watson and Westley 1958).

The term phase (rather than step) implies that each is part of a continual process rather than a series of separate interventions or events. Different kinds of interventions are normally required in each of these three phases. When choosing what to do, it is important to know what phase you are in.

The unfreezing phase involves developing a felt need to change within the organisation and moving it to a state of readiness to begin making the changes. The felt need to change may be triggered by external events, by painful experience (for example, malfunctioning in a specific area, intense criticism or pressure from within or without), by a vision of what others have achieved elsewhere, by information about current shortcomings, or by other planned and targeted interventions.

The amount of intervention required to unfreeze an organisation and move it into a state of readiness depends largely on the degree of resistance within it. For some organisations, this is where the major part of their equal opportunities effort needs to go. The data you gathered in chapter 2 will help you assess what your organisation needs.

Typical unfreezing interventions include an audit of existing practice, a survey of users to find out whether they have found services relevant and accessible, a brainstorming session in which staff say what they think equal opportunities is and how it relates to their mission, awareness training, and a special staff conference on equal opportunities and outputs. Think laterally about the kind of unfreezing interventions that will be effective in your organisation bearing in mind your aims, which are to open up the organisation to equal opportunities, to get people talking, and to assess their state of readiness.

The information you get during the unfreezing phase is important in helping you decide what steps to take next. You need information that is as accurate and comprehensive as possible, and to keep your plans flexible while continuing to focus on your overall objectives.

The moving phase begins only when the organisation and its key equal opportunities players are ready to change. Your aim in choosing suitable interventions for this phase is to implement the change programme, developing and stretching the capabilities of the people and the organisation to achieve your equal opportunities objectives and, ultimately, your equal opportunities vision. Typical interventions in this phase include any form of skill or knowledge-based training, on, for example, recruitment and selection, cross-cultural client interviewing, managing a multiracial team, setting up a disability project, counselling skills for advice workers on working with HIV positive clients. Other moving interventions include setting up working parties or task groups to develop codes of practice or guidelines, organising a team awayday on changing funding procedures in the light of the organisation's equal opportunities policy, and initiating programmes to train the board of trustees and internal trainers on equal opportunities issues.

The refreezing or institutionalising phase begins when both the organisation and the individuals within it have moved sufficiently towards the equal opportunities objectives. The time has now come to integrate equal opportunities permanently into the fabric of the organisation. This may involve spreading the change to other parts of the system which it has not so far been possible to involve in the change effort, establishing mechanisms or activities that will maintain the momentum of change, and ensuring that the structures and norms of the organisation support equal opportunities in the long term. It may involve, for example, setting up new reporting and accountability relationships, making corporate equal opportunities values explicit in the organisation's mission statement or partnership contracts, or setting up guardian angels within the organisation to guard the new culture and practices.

Other typical interventions in the refreezing phase include

incorporating equal opportunities responsibilities and accountability in job descriptions and in supervision and appraisal procedures, integrating equal opportunities thinking and practices into staff and volunteer handbooks, and setting up monitoring systems to assess the take up of new services from an equal opportunities perspective. The purpose of all refreezing interventions is to root equal opportunities in the formal structures and systems of the organisation, to move equal opportunities from being informal and discretionary to being formal, explicit and required. Even if all the equal opportunities change agents and the equal opportunities forums within the organisation disappear, equal opportunities will be from now on an integral part of its mainstream life.

The need for flexibility The phases outlined above and the interventions listed in each should be taken as a helpful way of thinking about change rather than as a rigid formula. Although it is always desirable, it is not always possible to proceed in an orderly fashion from one phase of change to another. For example, an organisation may be forced by tough external pressures to move forward without first unfreezing. All is not lost. It may be possible to push on and achieve the most urgent objectives despite the inevitable resistance and sabotage. Once these objectives have been achieved, the organisation can backtrack to do its unfreezing work by showing people why the old status quo is no longer acceptable.

Organisation L was put under urgent pressure by clients and funders to train advice staff in multicultural interviewing skills. Once this had been done and new practices had been implemented, the equal opportunities task force decided to take the advice staff and other key groups back through the logic of equal opportunities and why equal opportunities was vital to the achievement of the organisation's mission. This piece of backdated unfreezing work opened up new windows for change on which they were then able to capitalise.

Interventions that are normally part of the moving or refreezing phases can sometimes be used in the unfreezing phase, depending on the culture of the organisation and providing they are well-handled. For example, one voluntary organisation whose culture was extremely task-oriented was unfrozen by taking on equal opportunities tasks from the beginning. Carrying out these tasks boosted people's sense of achievement, lowered their resistance and prepared them for more change. In such an organisation, awareness training, for example, would have been entirely counterproductive.

How implementable is this intervention?

The best interventions are those that are *both* as effective as possible in helping you achieve your final equal opportunities vision (that is, that have the maximum 'strategic fit'), *and* relatively easy to implement, causing as little disruption as possible. Figure 15 shows the different possible combinations between strategic fit and ease or difficulty of implementation. As far as possible, you should try to choose interventions that are rated excellent, good or fair.

T, the person responsible for overseeing the implementation of equal opportunities in a national voluntary organisation, felt that the best intervention would be to develop a group of internal people to act as equal opportunities change agents. This would include internal trainers and consultants, and human resource people from both the national headquarters and the regional offices. All these people were very close to the practical day-to-day operations of the organisation. They also, between them, had access to all groups, from senior staff to grass roots field workers. Their combined skills, positions and influence within the organisation would make them ideal change agents.

However, when he considered this exciting plan in terms of its implementability, T identified major difficulties: the people in his chosen group were very resistant to development or training because they felt that as professionals they were already fully

Figure 15 Prospects for Different Interventions: implementability and effectiveness

Difficulty of implementation	High	Medium	Low
Low (Effectiveness)	poor	poor	poor
Medium (Effectiveness)	fair	good/fair	good
High (Effectiveness)	good/fair	good	excellent

Effectiveness in promoting equal opportunities (strategic fit) competent and informed. The head of training and development, based in the national office, and very influential within the organisation, made it clear that she thought equality issues were nonsense and completely irrelevant. She had already prevented the equal opportunities policy from being implemented within her department and had allocated minimum resources to it. There was also a history of competitiveness between the national team of trainers and the regional teams. Any idea of bringing them together to co-operate was generally thought to be hopeless.

Upon reflection, T decided that although his vision of an influential group of trained internal change agents sounded as though it would be highly effective and had a high level of strategic fit, the likelihood of it actually succeeding was extremely low. When another option came up, of working with three regional trainers and equipping them to design and deliver a pilot equal opportunities course, T decided to lower his strategic sights and go for greater implementability.

It is important to note here that this decision was not inevitable. Another change agent might have decided to try to go for the intervention with the maximum level of strategic fit, despite the clear difficulties of implementation. He or she could have decided to use the detailed analysis of the organisation to predict problems and to prepare as well as possible for them. Whether this intervention succeeded would depend also on the amount of energy within the organisation and on other factors in the situation.

How many dimensions must you take into account in planning each intervention?

Every change has several dimensions or focuses, for example, technical, political and cultural (see Figure 16), which must be taken into account when the change is being planned. For example, if you are introducing equal opportunities into your recruitment and selection processes, you need to take into account and manage:

Figure 16   Dimensions of Change

Dimensions of change

- Mission   ⎫
- Goals and plan   ⎪
- Structure   ⎪
- Technology and use of techniques   ⎬ Technical
- Tasks being done   ⎪
- Procedures   ⎪
- Regulatory systems   ⎭

- Leadership and authority patterns   ⎫
- Role definitions   ⎪
- Management style and practices   ⎪
- Impact on people   ⎪
- Decision-making processes   ⎬ Political
- External environment   ⎪
- Power groupings and aims of policy makers   ⎪
- Relationships between groups   ⎪
- Communication   ⎭

- Culture of the organisation   ⎫
- Norms and values   ⎪
- Staff qualities   ⎬ Cultural
- Other   ⎭

- the technical dimensions of the change—the use of different selection techniques, new procedures, new regulatory systems, etc;

- the political dimensions of the change—the decision-making processes involved, how the change will be communicated, who will be in favour of and against the change; and

- the cultural dimensions of the change—how the change and the way it is carried out fits into and will affect the organisation's normal way of working, its values, its culture and so on.

Every time you are considering an intervention, you need to consider which dimensions of your organisation are affected and how to handle each. Neglecting or ignoring important dimensions of the change will decrease your chances of success.

A voluntary organisation decided that it must have an equal opportunities policy because of demands from its funding bodies. A small working party was put together, chaired by a senior manager. He ruled the working party with an iron hand and made all the decisions about the way the policy should be implemented. It was decided that all staff must have recruitment and selection training and that each department must then draw up its own equality plan under direct guidance from top management. The external consultant went along with the programme because of her inexperience and the sheer speed at which the chairman moved the group. There was little time to think anything through.

After ten months the whole project fell apart because the departmental staff utterly refused to co-operate with the working party. They felt that the issue of equal opportunities had been hijacked by the chair, that the working party was not independent or creative, and that it had lost its credibility. As a result, not only did the equal opportunities programme fail, the organisation tore itself apart viciously and destructively, and took many years to recover.

A post mortem found that the whole of the change effort had focused entirely on the technical dimensions of change; the procedures, the tasks to be done, and regulatory systems. Important political and cultural dimensions, for example, management style and practices, power groupings, communication, relationships between groups, had been completely ignored. Looking back, the consultant realised that she had failed to help the group understand the complexity of managing change and the importance of taking less obvious dimensions into account.

How deep should you go?
The final set of criteria for considering any intervention is how deep it should go. How far should it penetrate into areas that are value-laden, emotionally charged, and central to people's sense of self, or to the organisation's core values and its culture? (Harrison 1970). In principle, a change programme should go no deeper than is required to produce lasting solutions to the problems being dealt with, and should ask no more than the energy and resources of the organisation and its people can cope with. An intervention that goes too deep or asks too much is likely to increase resistance and people's refusal to co-operate.

Resistance can manifest itself in surprising ways. It can lead to the development of extraordinarily sophisticated methods of discrimination and sometimes also closes all doors to future equal opportunities change. Some interventions, such as much racism awareness training, aim very deep, intruding without permission into people's most private and personal thoughts and feelings, and often causing unnecessary turmoil and resistance. Although this is very successful with some people, it is true that, in general, confronting people's racist and sexist attitudes does not guarantee change. In fact, if the process of confrontation has aroused anger or resentment, people may become more fixed in the attitudes the confrontation has uncovered and may even search for additional justification for them. Although it can be tempting to demonstrate publicly that people are wrong and to make them admit that their attitudes are unacceptable, particularly in an important cause, it can backfire dangerously in ways that cannot be predicted or contained. The change agent has a responsibility to use his or her skills to achieve positive change and to choose those methods that are most likely to be effective in doing so.

Deep intervention has a place in equal opportunities, but only if it is appropriately used and is essential in terms of the overall objectives. Many organisations have been pointlessly damaged by unnecessarily deep equal opportunities interventions, or by deep interventions that have been wrongly timed.

Possible problems

The last two sections of this chapter provide case studies and an exercise to help you decide your own plan of action. However, experience indicates that in many organisations, people's energy is often blocked at this stage because of worries about the money that may be involved in implementing an equal opportunities policy, or about how to deal with possible crises during the implementation programme.

Funding

If yours is a small and not well-funded organisation, you may feel disheartened by some of the case studies quoted in this book. Your organisation may not be able to afford an external consultant, an expensive training venue, or even the travel costs for a meeting. However, we hope that one of the messages you have gained from this book is that you do not have to do things in conventional or even obvious ways and that there is almost always a creative, alternative way round the problem. What relevant expertise do the staff and volunteers in your organisation have that you can draw on? Can you get new ideas through talking to another organisation that has been through the equal opportunities process? Can you cut costs by sharing facilities, administrative costs or even a consultant with one or more other organisations?

It may also be possible to slot equal opportunities initiatives in with other projects that decision makers are more ready to fund. For example, if output standards are slipping, client numbers are dropping, and staff morale is low, perhaps you can slot in equal opportunities as part of your revitalisation programme.

Crises

Implementing a programme of change is never completely straight-forward. There will always be some kind of setback or crisis, mainly because the context in which the change is occurring changes constantly.

121

It is important to anticipate possible crises and how they will be dealt with if they arise. Try to use a crisis, if at all possible, to strengthen your programme. Try to prevent it being weakened or, worse, subverted.

For example, if training has not gone well, call a representative group together to discuss why and get people to examine their awareness of their own resistance (even if the trainer was at fault); if a key working group member is leaving, think about bringing in two more people to take their place, or, if you can, arrange with their new employer to allow them to stay on the working group until the task is done, possibly offering the new employer some kind of compensation in kind; if piloting shows that your new code of practice is no good, get its vocal critics together to find out why. So long as you are absolutely clear about where you want to go and why, and about the ethical values that underpin what you are doing, you will find the confidence to use a crisis to improve your strategy.

Here are some general measures you can take in advance to help ensure that the crises that occur will not throw you off course:

- To ensure continuity in the equal opportunities programme, make sure that the people who are responsible for implementing the different parts understand and own their responsibility. Designate responsibility and accountability well in advance.

- Your ethics, core values and vision are your surest guides. Respond to crises in a way that is consistent with your basic beliefs and strategic vision. These will help you analyse accurately what has gone wrong and rescue the programme. Resist the temptation to cast blame or sling mud.

- Have a crisis management team (which can be the same as your equal opportunities task group) and ensure that it meets regularly to discuss potential problems and plan how to handle them.

- Anticipate that there will be threats both to your equal opportunities vision and to the organisation's ability to implement that vision. Discuss regularly with the key players what might go wrong and examine how they and the members of the task group would respond as individuals and in terms of the organisation.

Case studies

The case studies below show how the ideas set out so far were applied in a number of large and small voluntary organisations. Our intention is to give you a feel for the kinds of thinking and processes that organisations need to go through when working on equal opportunities. They are not presented as templates for you to follow, but as opportunities for reflection and learning.

The first four case studies show in detail how four different voluntary organisations planned and implemented their equal opportunities policies. Some of the initiatives they took were successful, others less so. Nevertheless, each organisation did the best it could, had a vision, worked hard at diagnosing and understanding the context in which it was making the change, and decided on interventions which seemed likely to be both effective and implementable. When they met failures or difficulties, they used what they had learnt to reshape their plan. The most important characteristics of all four organisations are their clarity about where they want to go and their commitment to getting there.

Family Service Units

The context
When Family Service Units (FSU) began to think about adopting equal opportunities in the early 1980s they were aware of how important equal opportunities issues were to their mission. They also knew that although they were doing good work in providing support for disadvantaged families and communities, they did not always reach black and ethnic minority families. There was pressure to take equal opportunities seriously both from senior management and from some

grass-roots workers. However, there was also a high level of general resistance within the organisation. Many of the staff felt that they were already achieving high professional standards of practice and that equality issues were therefore automatically being addressed.

In Mintzberg's terms (see Exercises 12 and 13) FSU is a professionalised bureaucracy with a flat, divisionalised structure. It is highly decentralised with very few layers of management. Its Quaker founding ethos means that FSU is deeply committed to democratic processes and to change by consensus; it is important that everybody should have a say and feel able to influence all decisions. There is also a strong feeling of professional autonomy. At the time when FSU embarked upon equal opportunities its staff were mainly white, female social workers, with a predominantly male middle management.

The unfreezing phase

FSU began by organising a staff seminar on equal opportunities with external speakers. This jolted the staff into thinking about equality issues and opened up a debate about the relevance of these issues to FSU. This was a relatively easy first-step intervention which did not go too deep but began to shift people.

FSU then joined forces with three other voluntary organisations and got external funding to set up an anti-racist consortium with a consultant whose function was to guide and support all four organisations in implementing equal opportunities.

The moving phase

FSU considered the following diagnostic information in deciding what interventions to use to move the organisation:

Vision and objectives   Race equality issues were the top priority. The key element of FSU's equal opportunities vision was to change its image and to make its services more accessible and relevant to black and ethnic minority families. The first step, therefore, had to be to change the staff profile to make it more representative and balanced in terms of the population it served.

Implementability and strategic fit The objective of a more representative and balanced workforce was a crucial issue of strategic fit, not simply an equal opportunities issue. With FSU's core mission of providing support for disadvantaged families, especially in inner-city areas, a staff that was 98 per cent white was clearly a problem. It was not that white staff could not offer a service, but that most of them had neither the language nor the cultural insight necessary to provide accessible and appropriate care to many of the families who most needed their support. In terms of strategic fit, therefore, the plan to change the staff profile was excellent. At the same time, FSU knew that there would be huge problems in trying to implement such a plan.

FSU headquarters needed to go against the organisation's decentralised structure and its culture of autonomy and change by consensus, and to make it a rule that staff who had not been through a three-day recruitment and selection training programme could no longer sit on an interviewing panel. This was the first time in FSU's history that such an edict had ever been issued, and everyone involved knew that going against the cultural grain in this way would cause major problems.

Dimensions of the change The first big step was to change recruitment and selection procedures and to produce a recruitment and selection manual which would bring the diverse practices of the 23 units around the country into line and ensure that new staff had the skills and abilities the organisation needed to achieve the equal opportunities objectives of this phase. It was essential to concentrate on the political and cultural dimensions of the change, for example, power groupings, security, relationships between groups, decision-making processes, and norms and values, as well as on the technical dimensions, for example, new procedures and regulatory systems.

Depth of intervention The proposals required intervention not just into the public area of how people carry out their jobs, but also into deep personal issues such as how people felt about their professional identity, how they felt about black people as clients and as colleagues, their loyalty to FSU's history and culture, and their sense of personal

125

and regional power and autonomy. This very deep intervention would arouse strong emotions.

Programme of action   FSU now began to work out the concrete steps they must take to achieve their equal opportunities objective. They chose a series of steps that would both mop up the unfinished part of the unfreezing phase and move the organisation as fast as it would allow. They knew they would have to work efficiently to achieve this ambitious programme.

- They set up a consultative forum to work with a senior manager on drafting the code.

- They spent six months on a consultation exercise holding workshops all around the country to discuss the draft code and its implications for staff practice. These enabled staff, many of whom were hostile to the changes, to voice their opinions. The people running the workshops (senior management and the external consultant) worked hard *both* at listening to this hostility *and* at confirming FSU's firm intention of going forward with the policy.

- There followed a long period during which all staff, unit local management committees, the trade union, and the black workers' and women's groups were asked to submit comments, suggestions and objections in writing to the consultative forum. The consultative forum then produced a document responding to every comment and criticism, explaining their responses, and setting out their own thinking as the group charged with leading the change. The document was circulated to all units for the attention of all staff, and to the unit local management committees. This was an effective intervention in itself and won over some of the positive resisters within the organisation. They respected the integrity of the group and the senior managers within it, and their professionalism in handling resistance.

- FSU then decided that in the next year it would spend over half its annual training budget on recruitment and selection. This sent a clear message that FSU was taking equal opportunities very seriously and was willing to put in the necessary resources to make it work.

- The consultative forum then considered who should do the training. They knew that in order to achieve the ownership that is essential for cultural change, particularly in such a decentralised structure, they must create and use internal change agents from the various units. These would also maintain the momentum of the change after the training and would eventually become guardian angels of the changes. They also knew that using internal people, whom participants could identify with and trust, would reduce resistance. They therefore decided to train internal people to carry out a massive three-day selection and recruitment course aimed at the whole organisation.

- The consultative forum wrote a person specification for the internal trainers and invited people to select themselves; 12 people came forward, some after a bit of persuasion. For them, one of the important benefits of being involved was that they also would develop new training skills which would be useful in their partnership work with external agencies.

- The external consultant from the anti-racism consortium worked with FSU's training manager and a senior manager in designing the course, and then all three together ran pilot courses with the volunteer trainers acting as observers. The volunteer trainers were able to learn from the courses without seeing themselves as being formally trained. A few of the volunteer trainers then tested the training material and adapted it to make it their own. This lengthy process produced 12 internal trainers each of whom was committed to running two or three recruitment and selection courses a year, working in groups of three. It also ensured their commitment not only to the training material but to the whole intervention.

- Within 18 months the whole organisation had been through the recruitment and selection training programme and there had been a major shift in attitude towards equal opportunities.

- During the training programme, FSU took a number of other steps towards their equal opportunities vision, including:

  - bringing in external trainers to work with senior managers and unit organisers on managing multiracial teams;

  - bringing in external trainers to carry out specialist training on, for example, integrating equal opportunities into all the external training carried out by FSU;

  - a one-day course for members of unit management committees;

  - a major discussion on equal opportunities issues at executive committee level; and

  - bringing other relevant procedures into line. For example, many units produced terms of reference for their management committee members stipulating that they must support all FSU's policies, including equal opportunities.

Results
The results of FSU's equal opportunities initiative included the following:

- In 1983 FSU had a predominantly white workforce. By 1993 the workforce was 25 per cent black.

- Equal opportunities became part of the culture of FSU. People no longer asked 'Why equal opportunities?', but only 'What?', 'When?' and 'How?'. Equal opportunities and anti-racist practice began to be entrenched in their everyday work.

- A number of innovative projects targeted at ethnic minorities were initiated, with the potential, in the long term, to influence social policy and practice nationally.

- A standing committee of the management committee (consisting of the chair of the management committee, the director of FSU, a union representative, and other staff) was formed to oversee equal opportunities issues. As a first step they produced an anti-racist statement to go with the equal opportunities policy.

- A monitoring group, chaired by an assistant director, was set up with formal responsibility for reviewing the code of practice every year and reporting to the national executive council.

- An assistant director was employed with a national policy brief to develop the agency's transcultural practice.

- All training courses were reviewed to check that they incorporated equal opportunities.

- New services were set up targeted at black and ethnic minority groups. Staff who spoke Asian and other languages were hired to work with people in those communities.

- Research on the Asian communities' experience of social policy was carried out and published. Funding was sought with other agencies to develop a network of Asian social policy researchers.

- Funding was obtained to develop a training programme over three years to increase skills in working across race and culture.

- Policies and codes of practice on anti-racism, sex equality and disability have been developed and will form a comprehensive 'equalities' package.

- The work programmes for two central projects on social policy and family support have as their central focus the impact of policy and practice on black families using FSU's services.

- The number of black trustees has increased as a result of a specific recruitment drive.

Gingerbread

The context

Gingerbread is a self-help organisation, founded in 1970, which aims to provide mutual support for lone parents. Its basic belief is that lone parents who are confident, supported and feel good about themselves make better parents than those who are lonely, unhappy and feel the victims of circumstances. Gingerbread works mainly through local groups, each of which is affiliated to Gingerbread and shares the same constitution. It also has some individual members who do not belong to a group. By the late 1980s, there were about 250 local groups and over 7,000 members.

In 1987 Gingerbread began to realise that equal opportunities, particularly in relation to race issues and to accessibility, was an important issue for them. Funding to develop an equal opportunities policy was obtained from the Joseph Rowntree Charitable Trust (JRCT). A project group to oversee the development and implementation of the policy was set up consisting of the director of Gingerbread, the development officer, the London worker and an external consultant.

In Mintzberg's terms (see Exercises 12 and 13), Gingerbread has a hybrid missionary divisionalised structure. Local groups are extremely autonomous, with the small national office providing only support, information and advice. Local organisers would therefore be the key players in implementing any equal opportunities programme.

The unfreezing phase

A number of initial diagnostic interviews were carried out by the external consultant. The interviewees, who included some national council members, staff members and parents from local groups, were asked about how they saw equal opportunities issues and their relevance to Gingerbread.

Two workshops were run, for staff and for national council members, on the importance of equal opportunities. The aims were to get support from the national council for the equal opportunities programme, and also to collect diagnostic information which would help in planning the next steps. This intervention was relatively easy to set up and did not aim too deep. Nevertheless, it created a sense of discomfort with the status quo within the organisation since it challenged people's personal feelings about equal opportunities in a non-confrontational way and called into question aspects of Gingerbread's culture. It also enabled the collection of useful data and opened up a debate on equal opportunities issues.

The project group was now ready to refine its plans for the next phase. At a one-day planning workshop the data collected so far were fed back to council members and staff. On the basis of these data and of the discussion that accompanied it, a plan of action was worked out.

Objectives and vision

The project group decided that the main aim of the policy should be to increase membership among black and ethnic minority lone parents by making local groups more accessible to them. Once that decision had been taken the specific means were clarified and refined:

- to produce national office guidelines on equal opportunities;

- to produce guidelines on equal opportunities for local groups;

- to train 12–16 representatives from local groups as facilitators to help people in local groups implement the equal opportunities guidelines;

- to provide training for national office staff; and

- to spread good equal opportunities practice through *Ginger*, the organisation's newsletter.

Gingerbread's vision was that at the end of the project:

- Fifty local groups would have participated in discussions on equal opportunities.

131

- Up to 10 local groups would have devised their own action plan on equal opportunities.

- Gingerbread's membership profile and the membership of its national council would be more representative of the national profile of lone parents.

- There would be a monitoring system to monitor the ethnicity of members and of groups.

It was clear that to gain access to local groups, it would be necessary first to achieve two things: to win the support and commitment of the democratically elected members of the national council, and to give Gingerbread's staff the skills and confidence to carry out the project. A preliminary action plan was developed taking this into account, though the project group realised that this plan would be refined and altered as the process continued.

The moving phase

The main thrust of this phase was to spread the message of equal opportunities to local groups, and to encourage them to become more accessible and welcoming to lone parents from different backgrounds.

Implementability and strategic fit   Gingerbread's original idea had been to run as many racism awareness workshops as the JRCT grant would allow, in order to increase members' awareness of racism and of how it operates. However, an analysis of the organisation revealed, among other things, that members were generally not at all ready to change on equal opportunities issues. Local members are lone parents coming together to give and get support, often in difficult circumstances. Racism awareness challenges people's deepest feelings and certainties in an uncomfortable and confrontational way. Unless it was preceded by targeted unfreezing events, such a deep intervention would be likely to scare members away and might close the doors of local groups to any further change. The equal opportunities project group decided that although the original idea had a high level of strategic fit, it would be very difficult and possibly even counterproductive to implement.

After some discussion the group decided to try an easier and gentler way of achieving the same objectives. They decided to produce a facilitator's manual on equal opportunities for use with local groups. This would aim to raise awareness of the link between self-help and equal opportunities, and would emphasise the benefits of equal opportunities in helping to attract new local members. Twenty-four facilitators would be recruited from local groups and would be offered training in conducting meetings and facilitating discussion, in using the manual, and on equal opportunities issues. They would help develop the equal opportunities manual for use with local groups. They would then go out to the groups and go through the manual with them.

Depth of intervention   Focusing members' attention on the needs of other lone parents who could benefit from Gingerbread's support network but were not currently doing so was a less deep intervention. It made a positive appeal to members' ideal of self-help for all lone parents. It also took into account and respected the relationship between the national office and the autonomous local groups. In addition, it provided an opportunity for some Gingerbread members to develop new skills. Other factors in the decision were the small size of the staff team compared to the number of groups and members, and Gingerbread's limited financial resources.

A great deal of thought went into how to present equal opportunities to the groups. Confrontation between the national office and the groups was to be avoided. It was important that everyone acting as a change agent should acknowledge and bear in mind four key facts:

- Groups already had established ways of operating which were important to them.

- Groups were struggling to survive because they lacked resources.

- Many members experienced a lot of stress in their daily lives.

- Members were as likely as most other people in society to be ignorant or misinformed about equal opportunities issues. However, this could be addressed through group discussion using the manual.

The action programme

The national office team   The external consultant met the national office team to find out about their roles and responsibilities and the way Gingerbread works. She then drew up draft equal opportunities guidelines for the national office and discussed them with the staff team before the final revision. It was felt that guidelines would be more useful than a rigid code of practice to help staff deal with the wide variety of enquiries, situations and tasks they deal with.

Local groups   A programme was set up to recruit and train local group facilitators to run equal opportunities workshops and to develop the manual. This required the external consultant to work very closely with the development officer and the London worker. The three did the following:

- Placed an article in *Ginger*, the organisation's newspaper, outlining the equal opportunities programme and inviting Gingerbread members to become facilitators. The article included a description of the skills and qualities required so that people could select themselves.

- Drafted an equal opportunities manual for facilitators.

- Ran a two-day residential training course for facilitators (with child care provided) on equal opportunities issues and facilitating skills. The facilitators went through the manual suggesting changes on the basis of their own experience. Training notes were compiled for the facilitators. The facilitators then set themselves targets for working with Gingerbread groups over the next year.

- Ran two follow-up support and training days for facilitators where they could report back on their experiences and review progress and needs.

- Ran a final evaluation meeting with facilitators where they also discussed the content and format of equal opportunities guidelines for local groups. The project group then produced these guidelines.

- Used Gingerbread's annual general meeting to reinforce the thrust of the policy through equal opportunities workshops.

- Ran a residential weekend for the facilitators to conclude this phase of the equal opportunities programme, to evaluate it and to plan the next steps for the national office and for the facilitators.

- Held a meeting with national office staff to report progress and discuss implications.

- Produced a final evaluation report with recommendations for the future for the Joseph Rowntree Charitable Trust and for Gingerbread.

Results

The results of Gingerbread's equal opportunities initiative included the following:

- Facilitators worked through the manual with representatives of about 50 groups in a variety of circumstances, including local group meetings, regional and county meetings, training days, and at the AGM. The target of 50 local groups participating in discussions on equal opportunities was therefore met but not in the way that was originally envisaged.

- Progress on the original vision statement that up to 10 local groups would have devised their own action plan on equal opportunities (see above) was more difficult to assess. The facilitators ran sessions for a large number of representatives from local groups who then took the issues back home for discussion. There was no formal system to monitor the outcome of these discussions.

- A voluntary monitoring system for both group and individual members was introduced in 1992. This produced a 25 per cent response rate. A question on disability has since been added.

- Equal opportunities guidelines for the national office were produced in consultation with staff members.

- Equal opportunities guidelines were produced for local groups, based on the equal opportunities project group's work with the facilitators and on the facilitators' own views. These are currently being distributed.

The future

Although local groups' response to equal opportunities issues has been generally positive, there has not been a major recruitment of black and ethnic minority lone parents into them. The organisation has come to the conclusion that it is possible that trying to recruit black and ethnic minority lone parents into existing groups is not the answer. Gingerbread is currently considering other experimental approaches, and is seeking funding to set up two regional outreach projects specifically targeted at black and ethnic minority lone parents. It has also designated an equal opportunities month to focus awareness among members and relaunch several equal opportunities initiatives. Since Gingerbread is still in the moving phase, there have been no formal refreezing actions so far.

The Save the Children Fund

The context

The Save the Children Fund (SCF) is, in Mintzberg's terms (see Exercises 12 and 13), a professional bureaucracy with a divisionalised structure. It carries out its mission through two operational arms; the overseas department and the UK department, each of which has regional offices which carry out its operations in the field. SCF also has several support service departments: fund raising, public affairs, and personnel and administration. Each of these has further subdivisions, forming a strong internal organisation.

SCF has a strong strategic apex based at the London headquarters, as well as a substantial group of middle managers who co-ordinate the professional staff out in the field. Staff in the field have a lot of specialist professional knowledge and expertise. There is an inherent tension between SCF's definitely hierarchical management structure and its professional staff's expectations of a more consultative approach. In addition, departments with very different roles, such as the UK and overseas departments, and the fund raising and public affairs departments, have different perspectives and subcultures and different ways of working. Their views on SCF policy and initiatives are often polarised. On the whole, the organisation manages to keep all these tensions in balance. Nevertheless, it was very important to take them into account in introducing an organisation-wide equal opportunities policy and programme of implementation.

The unfreezing phase

In 1923 the founder of SCF, Eglantyne E. Jebb, wrote a declaration, *The Rights Of The Child.* She included in it the right to protection 'beyond and above all considerations of race, nationality or creed'. In 1948 a revised version of Jebb's declaration became known as the *Declaration of Geneva.* Its principles form the basis of SCF's charter and work.

In the early 1980s, SCF decided to examine how well they were achieving the principles of their charter in their day-to-day work, and, in particular, whether their provision was 'beyond and above all considerations of race, nationality or creed'. SCF worked closely with a trade union, MSF, to produce an equal opportunities statement on employment policy. In 1984 a joint SCF-union equal opportunities working party was set up to appoint an adviser on personnel policy and to revise the employment policy statement. The same year, staff from a London-based SCF project, Building Blocks, presented their anti-racist work with under fives and their carers to a UK department's staff conference. All this focused many people's concern that SCF needed to examine and deal with the issue of racism within its structure and practices at all levels.

An anti-racism and multicultural policy development group was created and given the responsibility of producing a report for the UK department's committee. The group's terms of reference were:

- to review current structures, procedures and practices throughout the UK department (headquarters and field), to consider areas of concern, and to identify examples of sound anti-racist and multiculturalist practices;

- to review what other child care agencies, voluntary and statutory, have done and are doing in the field of anti-racism;

- to devise an anti-racism policy and to recommend

  - strategies for the implementation of the policy and

  - a means of monitoring the effectiveness of the policy throughout the UK department;

- to present an interim consultative document to the annual staff meeting; and

- to present a final report to the UK department committee.

In 1987, the anti-racism and multicultural policy development group published its report *Beyond and Above All Considerations of Race, Nationality or Creed*. This report was widely circulated internally. It influenced the decision to instigate a Fund-wide consultation which was a crucial step towards policy implementation at a later stage. The report had a significant effect on equal opportunities developments within SCF and, in July of the same year, SCF's highest decision-making body, the council of trustees, adopted an anti-racism policy and gave the responsibility for implementing and monitoring it to SCF's director general and directors.

Planning the programme
Specific responsibility for equal opportunities was given to a steering committee made up of the directors of the UK department, of the public affairs department, and of administration and personnel. They brought

in an external consultant to help them plan and initiate the process. The steering committee knew that such a complex organisation as SCF required a sophisticated approach. It was clear, for example, that a lot of time must be spent on the unfreezing phase since different departments had very different views on equal opportunities, and there was likely to be a high level of resistance among professional staff who would resent any implied questioning of the standards and value of their work.

Depth of intervention   The steering committee realised that in order not to close doors they should avoid too deep a level of intervention; the organisation did not have enough change agents to sustain the consequences of any deep intervention, and the culture was still very reserved and courteous with a powerful historical legacy. They also realised that simply issuing an anti-racism policy would not bring about effective long-term change. They planned to carry out the process of gaining group ownership gently, through people's participation in task groups.

Implementability and strategic fit   There are inherent difficulties in implementing any change throughout a large and complicated organisation, particularly one which operates in different countries and cultures. SCF is divided in terms of its operations, its functional expertise, its geography, professional groups, subcultures, history and politics. The steering committee accepted that implementing and achieving ownership of equal opportunities throughout SCF would be hard and would take time.

They therefore chose a programme with the highest possible level of strategic fit, that is, one that would deliver exactly what the organisation needed in order to achieve its equal opportunities objectives. They focused on one key service area, the UK department, and two key support service areas, public image and fund raising, and administration and personnel. (At that time it was difficult for a number of reasons to achieve change within the overseas department.) In addition, they went directly for lasting change in practice on the ground in these three key areas, rather than for training, workshops, or other less direct one-off interventions. And, instead of producing a general equal opportunities policy statement for the whole organisation, they decided to produce specific codes of practice and guidelines for each area. Finally, they decided to develop co-ordinated and coherent long-term implementation strategies and a maintenance plan.

Dimensions of change   The most obvious dimensions of change covered in the steering committee's plan were to do with tasks, procedures and regulatory systems. However, the process also involved other important dimensions such as people, decision-making processes, relationships between groups, and the culture and norms and values of the organisation.

The moving phase

The steering committee decided to set up a new structure to develop SCF's anti-racism policy. This would focus on achieving procedural changes through a widely representative forum, and would fit in with the way the organisation worked and with its culture. Three working groups were formed. These covered employment practice, fieldwork practice within the UK department, and SCF's public image and media presentation. All three groups would work under the guidance of the equal opportunities steering committee. Although the original impetus at SCF was on anti-racism, the final terms of reference for the working groups covered general equal opportunities issues, while focusing mainly on race.

The membership of the three working groups would be drawn from all the relevant sections of SCF, and would aim to reflect a balance of ethnic groups, genders, job types, levels of staff and management, and volunteers, and also to include people with special expertise or experience in equal opportunities issues. Having agreed these criteria, the directors decided that it was their responsibility to nominate the membership of the groups. This was acceptable in terms of SCF's culture and history.

Since the working groups would be large, would contain individuals from different parts of the organisation, and would deal with extremely emotive subject matter, it was important that they should be guided by very clear terms of reference. The terms of reference for the three working groups are set out below:

Terms of reference for the working group on employment practice

- To develop codes of employment practice covering, in particular, recruitment and training policies and their monitoring.

- To review the operation of procedures, such as disciplinary and grievance, and propose changes as appropriate.

- To understand the statistics available from ethnic monitoring.

- To develop and implement a strategy for the implementation of the codes of practice and any specific measures/initiatives which may need to be taken, including annual plans and targets for achievement.

The terms of reference also stated that 'it needs to be appreciated that membership of the group will demand a significant investment of time—probably on average one day a month, to cover the meeting times and preparatory reading'.

Terms of reference for the working group on fieldwork practice within the UK department

- To establish the nature of current professional practice within SCF, and perceived issues on which guidance and training are required.

- To establish principles of good practice:
  - in child care;
  - in working with local communities; and
  - in staff management;
  - and in how they can be monitored.

- To identify factors in the values and cultures of our staff, and of the people with whom we work, which are barriers to the full implementation of an anti-racist policy in the context of equal opportunities.

- To establish the training and learning needs of staff and propose strategies for meeting them.

- To facilitate and act as a co-ordinating group for divisional/local initiatives.

Terms of reference for the working group on public image and media representation

- To identify the principles which SCF's image should promote/reflect.

- To develop an understanding as to how corporate images are formed and examine the strengths and weaknesses of SCF's current image against the identified principles.

- To develop a strategy for projecting the desired image which takes appropriate account of the needs of such activities as fund raising.

- To review the existing image guidelines and propose changes.

- To develop an implementation plan which covers communications and guidance to committee members, branch volunteers, staff and supporters.

- To find out the public image policies of other UK and overseas child-care organisations, recognising that this could lead to the possible development of a code of practice among non-governmental organisations.

In order to help the members of the working groups see themselves as part of a larger movement of change, and to help them feel a strong sense of ownership of their tasks, a large introductory meeting was arranged for everyone involved. This launched the project and set out what was expected of it, provided visible, clear support and leadership from top management, laid down ground rules, and gave participants an opportunity to ask questions and raise problems.

Results

The equal opportunities working groups took 18 months to complete their tasks. Between them they produced:

- a revised equal opportunities statement for SCF
- guidelines on SCF's public image
- guidelines on UK fieldwork practice
- codes of practice for employment.

There was wide consultation within SCF on all four documents. The working groups, with the steering committee, then combed through all the responses, revised the documents and reported back on how they had dealt with the comments. SCF now had 35 people who had been through an intensive debate on equal opportunities issues, their relevance to SCF, and how equal opportunities should be put into practice in three specific areas.

The equal opportunities working group on fieldwork practice included people working at grass-roots level, professionals, administrators and managers. They developed their principles of good practice on the basis of their daily dilemmas and experiences. As a result these were practical and down-to-earth, full of concrete examples, though without being over-prescriptive, and very implementable. The principles were piloted in different sections of the UK department, in order to work out their implications for staff in each setting, and to see whether they were transferable in practice. Each section or project was then asked to develop their own practice guidelines based on the working group's principles. This approach involved another large number of people in piloting, discussing, and reviewing the principles and working on their own guidelines, thereby increasing awareness and ownership of the equal opportunities programme.

The public image guidelines produced by the working group on public image and media representation now influence all publicity,

143

fund raising, appeals, work with local groups and so on. They have been incorporated into SCF's corporate design and style guide and are used in internal training to encourage managers to become more conscious of the visual images they present in their work, and of the importance of giving fair and accurate representations of people of different communities. The guidelines are also respected and referred to by other agencies, and SCF has been asked to give several talks about how they were produced and implemented.

The equal opportunities working group on employment practice produced an 'Equal Opportunities Policy Statement and Code of Practice'. This established and codified good practice standards and processes which were implemented across the Fund for all UK-based staff. Once these had been in place for three years, further proposals were developed. Rather than produce one all-embracing code of practice, it was decided to develop a general policy statement for the whole organisation and then to ensure that all further employment policy development and casework incoporated equal opportunities as an essential component. The fruits of this approach have included a collective agreement on job security, a maternity leave policy and procedures, a policy statement on staff security and safety, and a policy and guidance document for dealing with complaints of harassment on grounds of race, sex, sexuality, disability, and religion. A monitoring group has also been established to collect, develop and interpret quantitative information on SCF's employment policy. At the time of writing SCF is also in the first stage of developing its human resource strategy as part of the overall planning process. Directors have agreed that this strategy should be 'values-based and objectives driven'. As part of this strategic development, each department will be asked to undertake a practical planning exercise to demonstrate what will be achieved on an annual basis in relation to equal opportunities in employment practice.

The refreezing phase
A final large meeting was held at the end of the project to celebrate and mark the end of the moving phase and plan the refreezing phase. The

three working groups presented what they had achieved, and discussed a strategy for maintaining the changes. A number of workshops were set up to discuss ways forward. Some of the refreezing actions they identified were:

- training and development to spread understanding and application of equal opportunities principles among a wider group of staff;

- a review of the costs and opportunities of a variety of monitoring systems, what should be measured, what constitutes success and so on, resulting in a practical monitoring programme;

- clarifying roles and responsibilities in relation to equal opportunities, examining who is responsible for implementing what, the impact of this on day-to-day work, and also management responsibilities; and

- exploring ways in which SCF could contribute to the efforts of other organisations attempting to implement equal opportunities.

Following this, a smaller group met to develop a programme of continuing action on equal opportunities at SCF. Progress is continuing, slowly but surely, achievements are being monitored, and further plans developed on the basis of those findings.

The British Deaf Association

The context
The British Deaf Association (BDA) was founded in 1890 by a Deaf[1] man, following an international conference of hearing educators who decided that sign language should be banned from schools teaching Deaf children. It brought together a group of volunteers and professionals from both the Deaf and hearing communities whose aim was to fight against this kind of prejudice and discrimination. The BDA

now has approximately 180 branches throughout the country. A branch has to fulfil certain criteria to become part of the BDA.

About ten years ago the first Deaf person was appointed as chair of the BDA and since then it has been led entirely by Deaf people. As a result of recent changes aimed at making the organisation more democratically accountable, BDA officials and trustees are now directly elected by individual members. Although anyone can be a member, only Deaf people are allowed to hold office.

The BDA has a chair, a vice-chair, and 21 trustees, all from the Deaf community, and 45 paid staff. It is managed by a team of senior managers led by a chief executive. Day-to-day operations are run by a second layer of managers. The organisation is physically dispersed: the head office is in Carlisle and is responsible for administration, finance, information, marketing, sign language services, advocacy and youth services. The chief executive is based in London, along with public relations, fund raising, interpreting services and the London Deaf Access Project. An education project and a health promotion project are both based elsewhere in London. The Crewe office specialises in health promotion and AIDS work, the Newcastle office runs a youth and advocacy project, and the Nuneaton office runs community advocacy. In Mintzberg's terms (see Exercises 12 and 13) the BDA is a missionary organisation with a strong strategic apex and a strong support function. Its culture has changed from a Zeus-type culture with an individual charismatic leader to that of a professional organisation, while retaining much of its visionary nature. Despite this structure the BDA has an open, consensus-management style.

The key areas of operation of the BDA are:

- sign language services including sign language interpreting services, projects to raise awareness of the nature and purpose of sign language, education, and expert advice on special cases and on government policies.

- advocacy mainly at national and European parliamentary level, also within the community and in individual cases, especially discrimination casework.

- youth work mainly to enable young people to become fully involved in the organisation and to become youth leaders and helping young people develop their full potential.

- information through a monthly national magazine for the Deaf community, a quarterly magazine for professionals, specialist information for different groups, working with the government and the public sector to ensure that crucial information reaches Deaf people, and promoting and producing videos as the main information medium for sign language users.

- health promotion especially increasing information within the Deaf community on AIDS and HIV, supporting and counselling Deaf people with AIDS or who are HIV positive, setting up support systems for carers of people with AIDS, work on alcohol and drug issues, victim support and 'well men and women' projects.

- education and training mainly working with parents of Deaf children to discuss educational needs and preferences, campaigning to improve provision, providing confidence-building and skills-based courses for school-leavers.

The origins of the pressure for equal opportunities

Two separate factors pushed the BDA towards the development and implementation of a comprehensive equal opportunities policy. The first was the appointment of a new chief executive whose vision was to strengthen the organisation and consolidate its achievements by developing its policies, procedures and structures. Until then, the BDA had been effective as a visionary organisation, driven forward by its missionary zeal and working effectively for the rights of the Deaf community in Britain. However, like many such organisations, its internal systems were informal, discretionary and individualistic. It had very few formal systems and procedures. The new chief executive saw equal opportunities as essential to the working of a strong effective organisation.

At the same time, the need to take equal opportunities seriously was fermenting steadily among some sections of the Deaf community. For example, five BDA branches were gay and lesbian clubs whose members were very much aware that although the BDA was totally committed to campaigning for the rights of Deaf people, it did not readily accept gay men and lesbians. These branches asked if they could air their views and concerns at the forthcoming BDA centennial conference in 1990. The BDA initially refused, but, following discussions with the chief executive and the senior managers, permission was given for the gay and lesbian clubs to hold a workshop. To general surprise, over 300 people attended the workshop, thus raising the profile of gay and lesbian issues and putting equal opportunities firmly on the BDA's agenda.

The unfreezing phase

The first step was to obtain agreement from council members for the organisation to launch a series of programmes to put its internal operations in order. The chief executive decided to raise members' awareness of the need for this through a skills and knowledge-based programme, using a course on recruitment and selection. The course was attended by council members and by all staff with a responsibility for recruitment and selection. It gently raised equal opportunities issues through a discussion of employment legislation and the rights of women, members of black and ethnic minorities, and disabled groups.

Following the course the BDA revised its recruitment and selection procedures, and set up a system to brief and raise awareness among other staff members and partnership agencies. The council gave permission for continued development and implementation of improved internal policies and practices under the banner of equal opportunities. This prepared the way for an extensive programme of action in the movement phase.

The movement phase

This phase was characterised by a highly implementable programme of change focusing mainly on technical dimensions. Although the overall programme of change chosen was very deep in terms of its overall impact on the BDA, the specifically equal opportunities aspect of the intervention did not aim unnecessarily deep.

Council members spent a day clarifying and setting out their roles and responsibilities, focusing particularly on equal opportunities issues. This enabled them to lead the major changes planned for the next few years from the front.

Council members and senior staff also had a refresher day on recruitment and selection processes, during which they explored equal opportunities issues further. This led to the setting up of a working party to develop the BDA's equal opportunities policy, headed by the director of information and made up of a representative group of staff. Its tasks include:

- producing an equal opportunities policy statement and the necessary codes of practice;

- establishing an equal opportunities monitoring unit (separate from the personnel function in order to ensure objectivity and maintain a broad focus);

- promoting equal opportunities to the whole Deaf community through positive leadership; and

- learning from the good practice of other organisations.

The equal opportunies working party produced a detailed policy statement and has begun work on detailed codes of practice. It was agreed that these would apply throughout the organisation and to all activities (not just recruitment and selection).

The BDA's existing ad hoc salary structure was overhauled using an organisation-wide job evaluation scheme. All job descriptions were revised, and an equal opportunities component was incorporated in each. This made the implementation of equal opportunities-based recruitment and selection procedures more effective.

The BDA then carried out an organisation-wide appraisal scheme with a view to setting up a training programme. A staff working group was set up to develop and implement the scheme, incorporating equality outputs and practices in the appraisal. This development met with general support from all heads within the organisation.

All staff-related matters, including terms and conditions of employment, were formalised through codes of practice in a new staff handbook. This enabled the BDA to incorporate equal opportunities issues throughout. A joint staff consultative forum was set up to handle negotiations between staff and management. A new recruitment and selection package was produced.

The BDA then began the process of developing a policy and code of practice on internal communication, looking at the crucial issue of making information accessible to all members, trustees, staff and volunteers, whether Deaf or hearing. This is vital to the successful achievement of equality practices and outcomes within the BDA since up till then some information had been more accessible to hearing groups and people with good English skills and other information to Deaf groups.

The BDA has also, at the time of writing, begun to address the integration of equal opportunities into the services it delivers, through service audits and a number of positive action projects. These include:

- A quality assurance project in which all staff involved in service delivery carry out an audit of services to ensure that BDA services are delivered to an agreed and clearly publicised standard. There is a strong commitment among those involved to ensure that BDA services are relevant and accessible to everyone within the Deaf community. Equality targets, values and practices are built into the audit scheme.

- A youth-based project in Coventry to reach out to Asian Deaf people.

The next steps are to integrate equal opportunities into other organisational development work within the BDA, including communications and quality assurance.

An organisational development analysis of the BDA's programme

After 100 years of an outward-focused missionary approach to its work, the organisation needed to focus its attention inwards, consolidating and strengthening its internal operations to ensure that it could sustain and build on its achievements. The development and implementation of equal opportunities were part of this process. A major advantage of this approach was that it took into account the BDA's energy and capacity for major change. The organisation would not have been able to sustain both a rigorous internal consolidation programme and a separate radical equal opportunities programme. It was also important for the organisation not to make changes faster than it could sustain them. Making major equal opportunities changes without a strong internal organisation is like building on sand.

Subsuming equal opportunities under the process of making the BDA stronger meant that the level of specific equal opportunities intervention did not have to be too deep. Ownership of equal opportunities was obtained by appealing to the missionary commitment of potential resisters. By taking equal opportunities out of the political arena, the BDA also built a strong base for the next phase of equal opportunities development. The results of the most important equal opportunities achievements will therefore only become clearly visible in the next phase. In OD terms this was a strong approach even though it is recognised that the different groups that fall under the banner of equal opportunities have not yet received the separate attention they will eventually need.

Once the equal opportunities working party has completed its work, the BDA will be able to evaluate critically its achievements so far and to identify what is still needed to achieve its equal opportunities vision.

The above case studies focus in detail on how four organisations approached equal opportunities as a major piece of development, using their understanding of their own organisations and applying clear criteria in deciding how best to proceed. Although the thinking with

151

which each organisation approached the process of introducing and implementing equal opportunities was similar, the four organisations are very different in terms of history, size, structure, level of complexity, culture and so on, and this dictated their different practical approaches. Your own organisation is different again, and must be the key factor that dictates all the decisions you make on how to introduce and implement equal opportunities within it.

The two short case studies in the rest of this section each highlights a specific innovative action taken by a small voluntary organisation and illustrates the need to think innovatively and imaginatively about what will best meet the specific needs of your organisation.

Contact a Family

Contact a Family is a relatively new charity set up in 1979 to provide support to families with children suffering all types of disability. It works through 500 locally-based parents' groups and over 300 national groups. Parents often belong both to a local group of parents of children with a range of conditions, and to a national group of parents of children with a particular condition. Contact a Family's local community projects have given emphasis to the importance of equal opportunities and have published a number of reports.

Each parents' group has its own management committee. The rules for a group wishing to be affiliated with Contact a Family are simple and take up only one sheet of A4 paper. It is here that Contact a Family has taken an important step in spreading the message of equal opportunities. To be affiliated, groups must pay a fee, register with Contact a Family, mention their affiliation on their note paper and use the charity number. In return they are asked to:

- stay in touch so that Contact a Family can pass on up-to-date information about them to other parents

- keep their financial affairs open and above board

- operate equal opportunities principles within their group. What this means in explained simply in the rules.

This first step was simple, not too painful, but very important in spelling out the mutual expectations of the national office and the local groups. Provided this step is followed by outreach work carried out by experienced development officers and by regular monitoring, it has the potential for creating a healthy network of independent parents' groups under the Contact a Family umbrella. For some organisations, an apparently simple action is a logical first step towards further change.

Contact a Family has an established equal opportunities statement of principles and an equal opportunities committee which meets quarterly. In addition Contact a Family aspires to be an equal opportunities employer and has established equal opportunities procedures for selection and recruitment to all vacancies.

A small volunteer-based organisation

Very few organisations whose services rely mainly on volunteers have taken steps to ensure that their recruitment and selection of volunteers take equal opportunities principles into account. Here is an example of one that has:

When two of the staff in this small organisation first raised equal opportunities issues in relation to the recruitment, selection, training and support of volunteers, they came across a good deal of resistance from both organisers and some members of the board of trustees. Other staff also wondered why such a fuss was being made about equal opportunities. As a preliminary unfreezing move, and to begin to unblock resistance, a one-day course run by an external consultant was organised for staff and board of trustees members on auditing the organisation's philosophy and its approach to volunteering.

During this carefully structured day, participants were asked to reflect upon their vision of volunteering and their commitment to it. As they reflected, it became clear to them that the way they currently recruited and placed volunteers did not fit in with either their vision or their goals. Although the day was not specifically about equal opportunities, issues of social justice and inequality were inevitably raised during discussions. As a next step, two volunteer organisers, the general secretary, a member of staff and a board of trustees representative rewrote their approach to volunteers, based on the discussions and conclusions that had emerged.

An innovative recruitment programme was then set up which enabled the organisation to change the profile of its volunteers from almost entirely white women, to both men and women of different ethnic groups and all ages. The organisation then had to cope with inducting and supporting these new kinds of volunteers and trying to ensure that the people and organisations with whom they were placed were not overtly or subtly harassing them. At this point, the staff responsible for these areas asked for further training and development on equal opportunities. The training took place with no resistance at all, and staff were then ready to venture into further unknown territories.

Although there were inevitable conflicts throughout the process, the results of this programme were significant. The organisation now has direct links with black and ethnic minority communities, and with groups of people with disabilities, where they now hold training sessions on personal effectiveness so that people who would like to volunteer can decide where they would be most effective.

The experience of this small organisation demonstrates the kinds of intervention that can be taken to improve volunteer profiles. In this case, the sheer weight of resistance from the volunteer organisers led people to use a 'moving phase' type of intervention, the innovative recruitment programme, to unfreeze the organisation. The volunteer organisers then came back to ask for backdated 'unfreezing work'. It was important for those heading the change towards equal opportunities to remain clear throughout about their original vision.

Deciding what steps you need to take

Although there are many valuable lessons to be learnt from other organisations, in the end every organisation must chart its own journey. The following exercise will help you decide what kinds of intervention are most appropriate for you.

Exercise 21 Deciding What Steps You Need to Take

Aim: To review the possibilities and decide which interventions are most appropriate for your organisation, and in which order.

Instructions: Discuss the following questions with your colleagues. Make sure that everyone has read this chapter first and ask them to bring with them a list of the issues that concern each of them about moving into the intervention stage. Work through all the questions below, bearing in mind everything you have learnt about your organisation and about the processes of change up to now, and bringing in the issues that concern each of you. Note down all the possible interventions that come to mind as you go. (The order in which the questions are set out is not significant. Consider them in any order that suits you.)

- Where do we want to get to? What interventions will best fit in with our overall equal opportunities strategy, that is, what interventions will have the best strategic fit?

- What are the main factors affecting the implementability of any programme in our organisation? How does each intervention rate in terms of implementability?

- Is it helpful to think about the process up in terms of unfreezing, moving and refreezing phases?

- What dimensions of change do we need to focus on for each intervention? (see Figure 16)

- Which interventions are more suitable for achieving short-term changes, to trigger further change, and which are more suitable for achieving and institutionalising lasting long-term change?

- How does our list of concerns affect our choice of interventions?

- Who needs to own each of these interventions for them to succeed? How can we achieve this ownership?

155

When you have finished, discuss your findings together and work out a detailed programme of interventions in sequential order. Work out for each intervention what will be needed to enable it to happen, for example, getting permission or approval, consulting or involving key people, preparations, training and so on. Then agree a reasonable schedule of implementation.

Debriefing: In some ways the kind of intervention you decide upon is less important than its purpose and how it fits into the context of your organisation. You need to retain confidence in the fact that if you are clear about where your organisation is *now* and where you want it to be in *the future*, there are many routes you can take. As long as those routes are sensible and well-managed, the exact details of their form and shape are less important. No one has ever mapped out and travelled a 'perfect' route to equal opportunities. What matters is that you apply everything you have found out, stick to your vision and your principles, and travel a route that makes sense to you. Then there will always be enough energy to get you through to the end, despite inevitable problems and mistakes on the way.

You have now reached the point where your plans can take off and your hard work will finally reap its rewards. Congratulations!

Chapter 6
Evaluation–Measuring Success and Updating Your Strategy

Evaluation is a programme of practical activities to measure the progress of equal opportunities within your organisation. In organisational development (OD) theory, evaluation is also an important intervention, a powerful part of the process of change, rather than an end in itself. As you begin to evaluate progress and feed the data back, people's understanding of equal opportunities issues and practices will further increase. This, and the celebration of the successes you discover, will nourish and support the continuing equal opportunities programme.

You need to keep asking questions like 'What will this actually mean in practice?', 'How will we know when we have achieved it?', and 'What will the milestones be along the way?'. The answers to these questions provide the basis for your evaluation programme. Planning your evaluation from the beginning also ensures that your objectives for the whole programme of change are clear.

This chapter concentrates mainly on the potential impact that the evaluation process can have in shaping and steering the process of change, rather than on the methodology of evaluation.

The nature and purpose of evaluation

Any organisation undertaking a major programme of change needs to carry out systematic evaluation to find out whether the objectives of the programme are being met, the effects of the changes, and what more needs to be done to ensure the programme's ultimate success.

As an OD intervention, evaluation also achieves the following:

● It forces people to define the objectives of the change programme.

● It forces people to define the expected outcomes and how they will be measured.

● It forces them to spell out clearly how certain procedures, events and activities will be carried out.

● It helps to alert people to many of the problems that are likely to arise during the change programme.

● It helps people plan the next steps for their organisation (Burke 1982).

In reality, there is usually more talk than action when it comes to evaluation. Everyone agrees that they ought to evaluate, but very few actually do. The pressures against evaluation in the voluntary sector should not be dismissed lightly. They include work overload, lack of planning, a feeling that because the organisation is 'doing good' formal evaluation is unnecessary, unclear definition of the objectives of a change programme, lack of experience and lack of confidence. Lack of confidence is particularly important; many people think of evaluation as complicated, highly technical, full of jargon and mystery and much too difficult to attempt.

In actual fact there need be nothing complicated or mysterious about evaluation. It is simply a series of practical, common-sense steps which enable the people driving and involved in the change process to tell whether they are on the right track. The more that people within your organisation get involved in different bits of evaluation and understand its purpose, the sooner they will see it as a perfectly normal and useful activity.

At the same time, it is important for those people responsible for planning and organising evaluation to remember that it is never simply a straightforward technical task. For a start, it always has political aspects (Rossi, Freeman and Wright 1979). There are always groups and individuals both inside and outside the organisation with an interest in what is being evaluated and how, as well as in the results and how they are used. Evaluation is also affected by the context in which it is carried out. An organisation's structure, its culture and many other factors all have an impact on the types and quality of evaluation carried out, and on the ways the results are handled and used. You need to consider, for example, how to make sure that your findings will be credible to key groups, what areas of evaluation will be particularly important in view of your organisation's mission, and what methods of evaluation will be both reliable and acceptable in terms of the way your organisation works.

The most important things to bear in mind in planning your evaluation programme are:

- Evaluation should be a collaborative exercise in which everyone involved has an opportunity to voice and discuss their views and play a significant part, however small, in planning, designing, executing and/or analysing the findings.

- The evaluation process should stick strictly to its stated objectives and criteria. Other objectives should not normally be introduced once the evaluation process has begun or, worse, during the analysis of results.

- The methods of evaluation you choose should take into account the capacity of your organisation and the constraints on it. They should be practicable and should not put too much strain on those who have to carry them out. What matters is not the volume of data you collect but that it should be the right data.

- Evaluation should provide clear data on which to base decisions about what to do next to further the change process.

What to evaluate

There are five main areas of equal opportunities change to evaluate. You need to look at all of them to be sure that you have a complete picture.

1 The overall equal opportunities programme

How far has it progressed towards its stated objectives? How has it affected the practices, behaviour, thinking and values of the organisation? Has it achieved its vision?

2 Specific practical tasks achieved

These are the practical tasks set out in the equal opportunities policy and programme of action. They may include, for example, writing codes of practice, integrating equal opportunities into the induction programme for staff and volunteers, or publishing a disability awareness booklet. Each of these should be evaluated against the criteria set out for it when it was planned.

3 Equal opportunities projects and programmes

These may include, for example, a positive action programme, a translation and interpreting service, a new campaign targeted at a particular group, or a training programme for staff and volunteers. Again, each of these should be evaluated against the criteria set out for it when it was planned, and the reasons for any problems investigated. For example, has the project achieved its stated objectives? Has the training changed attitudes and behaviour as required? If not, why not? Was the initial analysis of needs inadequate? Was the programme poorly thought out? Was the trainer at fault? Was the resistance to change among certain groups far more entrenched than you had realised?

4 Key people

Has the equal opportunities programme changed the way groups or individuals do their jobs? Do they understand the reasons for the changes? Are they able to apply their understanding to new tasks and areas? What is their attitude to equal opportunities? Are they now taking equal opportunities initiatives and making changes for themselves? Positive answers to these kinds of questions indicate that equal opportunities is seeping into the thinking and culture of the organisation.

5 The change process

How do people feel about the way the process of change has been handled? What can be learnt from the responses of different individuals and groups to the changes? What did they find particularly difficult? What did they welcome? Did the predicted conflict occur? How well was it handled?

Although in the long term you need to evaluate *all* these areas, in the early stages of an equal opportunities programme it is important to be realistic about what is likely to have been achieved. At the end of the first year, for example, in which most energy will have been spent on the 'orderly tasks' it is realistic mainly to evaluate the achievement of these. You may also be able to evaluate the beginnings of a fairly straightforward new project such as equal opportunities training for volunteers, or a new induction programme. More complicated projects may take several years to produce results. Similarly, at the beginning it is only reasonable to look for changes in people's job-related performance. It takes a lot longer to achieve changes in attitudes and to see people begin to take their own equal opportunities initiatives.

There is, however, one area in which evaluation must be carried out consistently and from the beginning: people's views of the change process itself. It is very important that those in charge of the equal opportunities programme get regular feedback about how the changes are going and how people are reacting to them. This information can then be used to modify or add to the implementation programme where necessary and to plan further changes.

The programme of evaluation that was proposed at Gingerbread used each of the five areas described above.

Evaluation at Gingerbread

A crucial feature of Gingerbread's equal opportunities programme was the very clear definition of its objectives (see p. 131 above). This made it relatively easy to decide what to evaluate.

The overall equal opportunities programme

The overall aim of the project was to increase membership among black and ethnic minority lone parents by making local groups more accessible to them. To evaluate progress towards this aim Gingerbread needed to know the membership profile at the beginning of the project and to decide what percentage increase in the numbers of black and ethnic minority lone parents they were aiming to achieve by when. They also needed to work out what being more accessible would mean in practical terms, and to develop a set of indicators to measure this.

Specific practical tasks achieved

These included national office guidelines on equal opportunities, guidelines on equal opportunities for local groups, an equal opportunities policy statement for the whole organisation, and revised affiliation and membership forms. The evaluation programme focused on whether and how these tasks were done, and on the quality and usefulness of what had been produced.

Equal opportunities projects and programmes

The main project for Gingerbread was to help people in local groups implement equal opportunities guidelines, and to do so by training 12-16 group members as facilitators to work with groups around the country. The evaluation programme focused on the number of facilitators who had been trained, what they had learnt, whether they were effective in working with local groups, what changes they had achieved with local groups, whether the materials produced were relevant and effective, and so on.

Key people and the change process

This required an investigation of the views of national office staff and of the facilitators and also of their performance in the target areas. For example, did national office staff understand the logic of equal opportunities for Gingerbread and could they explain it to other people? Did they automatically implement equal opportunities values and practices and the equal opportunities guidelines in the areas for which they were responsible? Did the facilitators understand the logic and benefits of equal opportunities for Gingerbread and its members and potential members? How effective were they in facilitating discussion about equal opportunities and in helping people to implement changes in local groups?

It was also important to think carefully about timing. For example, in the first year the evaluation programme concentrated on the specific practical tasks set out in the implementation programme, and on the first stages of the main project. It also monitored people's reactions to the whole process and used their findings to fine-tune the programme. Being clear about what it is useful to evaluate and when helps in the development of a manageable evaluation programme and prevents the organisation becoming overwhelmed.

Exercise 22 Deciding What to Evaluate

This exercise helps you develop an evaluation programme for your own organisation. It is important to do this as part of the same process as planning the implementation programmes in chapters 3 and 4. Working out in advance what aspects of the implementation programmes should be evaluated, and what your indicators of success will be, both ensures that you think very clearly about the changes and enables you to set up evaluation methods and systems which will disrupt the day-to-day workings of the organisation as little as possible.

Aim: To decide what should be evaluated and when.

Instructions: Draw Chart 8 on a large piece of paper. List each of the areas you want to evaluate under the five categories on Chart 8. Your evaluation plans for years 1 and 2 should be fairly definite. Those for years 3, 4 and 5 can be less so at present.

Looking at each of the specific areas you want to evaluate, discuss and note down:

- What do we want to know or measure here?

- What criteria will we use to assess success? Are there external criteria (for example, in an EOC or CRE document) we could use? Do we need to take different people's or groups' criteria into account? What should we do if there is a conflict of opinion?

- What evaluation methods should we use for this, eg questionnaires, interviews, observation, monitoring? Whom should we ask or observe? What should we count?

- How detailed should our evaluation be and at what level, eg individual, team, unit, whole organisation?

- What will we do with the findings?

Debriefing: In years 1 and 2 it is likely that most of your evaluation will focus on specific practical tasks and on people's views about the change process.

As time passes, your evaluation programme needs to concentrate increasingly on assessing the impact of equal opportunities on the whole organisation and its outputs, how far the organisation has moved towards its original equal opportunities vision, and whether equal opportunities can be shown to be part of its culture.

Chart 8 What to Evaluate and When

Area of evaluation / Years	Overall EO programme	Specific practical tasks	Projects & programmes	Key people	Change process
Year 1					
Year 2					
Year 3					
Year 4					
Year 5					

Who should be involved in the evaluation?

It is important to involve everyone who can offer valid information in the evaluation process. This should include:

- decision makers
- people involved in carrying out the changes
- the change agents
- people affected by the changes.

Some will help decide the criteria to be used, others will be interviewed or monitored, others will be asked to read and comment or act on the results.

Decision makers

These are likely to include the board of trustees and senior staff, that is, the people who must be seen to own and lead the equal opportunities policy, and who have the power to allocate further resources to equal opportunities initiatives. Among other things, they want to see that the effort, time and money the organisation is putting into equal opportunities are producing tangible results in terms of cutting staff turnover, saving money, increasing the numbers of service users, improved public image and so on.

People involved in carrying out the changes

These are the people who are trying to make equal opportunities happen within the organisation. They may be, for example, the people who have to follow the new codes of practice or guidelines in their everyday work, people who have been trained in new skills or are working in new situations, those who arrange or run positive action programmes and so on. Their interest lies more in the results of the specific programmes or projects in which they are involved.

The change agents and members of the equal opportunities task group

The people overseeing and planning the whole process of the introduction and implementation of equal opportunities play a very important role in the evaluation process. They need to see the whole picture, taking into account the impacts of the various interventions on behaviour, attitudes, organisational procedures, relationships, culture and so on, and the achievement of a healthy, functioning organisation. They also need to decide whether any major or minor changes need to be made in the whole equal opportunities programme, to identify unexpected areas of difficulty and to decide how these should be managed.

People affected by the changes

These are the people whom the changes are intended to benefit, for example, black and ethnic minority cancer patients, disabled tenants in a new housing initiative, women managers who have taken part in a positive action training and development programme.

It is important to involve all these groups in some way. Each plays a different role in the process of change and each brings a different perspective to evaluation. However, there must also be one named group (normally the equal opportunities task group) which takes overall responsibility for driving the whole evaluation process, deciding how it will be carried out and whom to involve.

In such a highly-charged area as equal opportunities, the decision on which individuals to involve in each part of the evaluation process can be difficult. Working out *what* needs to be evaluated first makes the decision on *who* should be involved easier. Try to select people strictly on the basis of the objectives of the evaluation programme and of the overall equal opportunities policy objectives. This will help you ensure the credibility of the final results and avoid accusations of bias.

Exercise 23 Deciding Who Should Be Involved

Aim: To decide who should be involved in each piece of evaluation and how.

Instructions: Draw Chart 9 on a large piece of paper. For each specific area listed on Chart 8, discuss the following questions:

- Who should or could be involved in the evaluation of this area and why?

- In what way should they be involved, for example, carry out interviews, be interviewed, design or fill in a questionnaire, put questionnaire or interview findings together, and/or sit on the equal opportunities evaluation panel?

- What kind of evaluative information might this individual or group be interested in?

- Do they have time to be involved? Are they sufficiently interested?

- What is the best way to get them to take part?

Note your conclusions on Chart 9.

Debriefing: It is important to work out who is most able to provide full and accurate information on the areas you wish to evaluate, and also, among those who are less vital to the process, who is keen to be involved and who is not. If you have too many candidates you need to handle the selection process sensitively and carefully so that people who are not formally involved understand your decisions and do not feel excluded.

How to evaluate

The most important criterion for evaluation is to keep it simple. Your aim is to find out reliably and without too much effort and disruption

Chart 9 Deciding Who Should Be Involved

Area to be evaluated	Who should be involved?	Doing what?	Key data for them?	Time? Interest?	Final decision on who will be involved
1					
2					
3					

how things are going and what to do next. This is not the moment for heavy statistical exercises with convergent and discriminant validity etc. Nevertheless, if evaluation is an area with which you are unfamiliar, you may find it useful to refer to a comprehensive and practical book on evaluation.

Here are three simple and effective methods of evaluation:

Statistical monitoring

This is useful for measuring the outcome of a specific intervention or programme. For example, to find out whether a recruitment drive targeted at disabled people is successful, monitor the number and proportion of disabled applicants for jobs and the number of successful disabled appointees. To discover whether a special initiative to reach women who are HIV positive is succeeding, count the number of women seeking the service over a specific period. There may be an existing system which can be adapted for monitoring. This will make it easier to introduce.

Questionnaires and interviews

These are usually directed either at receivers of services or at people in the organisation who are implementing the changes. The choice of interviews or questionnaires will depend partly on how much qualitative information is needed (for which in-depth interviews are generally better), and partly on how much time is available and where the people to be surveyed are. If all the organisation can manage within its resources is a short multiple choice questionnaire and you think it will achieve your evaluation objectives, go ahead. It will be a lot better than nothing.

Observation

This demonstrates in a very straightforward way what is actually happening, for example, how counter staff behave with non-traditional clients, how volunteers relate to black and ethnic minority children. It is important first to work out agreed objective criteria with those concerned so as to avoid charges of subjectivity, bias and so on.

The voluntary sector has not yet begun to explore the many creative ways in which evaluation can be carried out. There are many ways in which people can evaluate progress and get information about what is and is not working, while, at the same time, becoming more involved in and committed to the equal opportunities programme. Although the choice of evaluation methods is important, do not be overwhelmed by the technical complexities. Regard evaluation simply as another intervention which must be based on careful thought and accurate information. Be clear about the objectives of the project and of your evaluation, and about the individuals and groups you need to influence. Here is an example of how one voluntary organisation evaluated a part of their equal opportunities programme using methods that were simple, participative and informative. Enjoy yourselves!

One plank of Organisation P's equal opportunities programme was that all national office training and personnel staff should take on responsibility for facilitating equal opportunities changes within the organisation as internal change agents. In practical terms, this meant that all the training and personnel staff were required to develop a comprehensive understanding of equal opportunities issues and their relevance to the organisation, and to produce an open learning package on equal opportunities issues for staff and volunteers.

The evaluation programme had four parts;

- *task evaluation*, that is, whether the package had been produced, how useful and accessible it was, whether it was being used, and whether the necessary support was provided for users. The equal opportunities task group, in consultation with the people involved, decided to ask potential users to rate the package using a checklist of agreed criteria, and to get the people who produced the package together to discuss

171

whether it met their own criteria for success and what they had learnt during the process. They also considered setting up an editorial task group to work with the people producing the package to evaluate progress from the beginning.

- *user evaluation*, finding out what users had learnt from the package, whether they had found it easy and pleasant to use, whether they had had enough support, whether they were allowed enough time in which to study, what improvements they would suggest. This was evaluated by a short questionnaire sent to all users followed up by a number of more detailed interviews. The questionnaire and interviews were based on the criteria of success agreed at the beginning.

- *training and personnel staff's evaluation*, finding out how they found the process, whether they enjoyed working on the package, what they learnt, and whether they now feel confident and articulate to discuss equal opportunities issues internally and in public. A structured follow-up and development day was held for this group in which their experience was discussed and further equal opportunities strategies planned for themselves and for the organisation.

- *manager's evaluation* The person in overall charge of the equal opportunities programme drew up a brief report summarising all the above findings and assessing the success of the project against criteria that had been drawn up beforehand. This was presented to the assistant director of administration and personnel who had approved and funded the project out of her budget.

Chapter 7
Developing an Equal Opportunities Learning Culture–Keeping the Momentum Going

A number of social scientists (Garratt 1987; de Geus 1988; Senge 1992; Stata 1990; Nonaka 1991; Myers and Davids 1992; Pearn and Kandola 1993) have recently become curious about why some organisations respond well to and maintain the momentum of major change, while others respond badly or fail to follow it through. Their key conclusion is that for an organisation to survive in times of change, it and the individuals within it must keep learning—from experience, from their external environment, and from their mistakes. And that they must keep using what they learn to adapt themselves to deal with a complex and changing world. 'Learning organisations' must also sustain and keep building on the changes they have achieved, so that new approaches and practices do not become fossilised but are continually adapted to meet changing circumstances.

These findings are crucial to the difficult and complex area of equal opportunities. Although, once you and your organisation have embarked upon the implementation of equal opportunities, you will have achieved an amazing amount, you will not have finally arrived. To ensure that you can maintain what you have achieved, and continue to learn and develop, your organisation needs to become a learning organisation.

What is a learning organisation?

A learning organisation is one 'where people continually expand their capacity to create the results they truly desire, where new and expansive patterns of thinking are nurtured, where collective aspiration is set free, and where people are continually learning how to learn together (Senge 1992:3).

Learning organisations are likely to display the following features:

- They take every opportunity to learn both from experience and in general at individual, team, and organisational level.

- They experiment with new ways of organising work and new ways of learning both within and outside the organisation.

- They establish a climate in which learning in general and learning from each other are supported and actively encouraged.

- They use training to support and facilitate the development and learning of all employees.

- They see a primary role of management as enabling people to manage themselves in groups and to acquire greater autonomy.

- They develop a structure which encourages two-way communication as a vehicle for learning and development.

- They encourage questioning, experimentation and exploration of new ideas and opportunities at all levels in the organisation.

- They remove barriers and blockages to learning in both the individual and the environment.

- They encourage and foster continuous learning and self-development and the necessary skills in all employees, not just in managers and directors.

- They recognise that individuals often learn effectively in groups and encourage project-based and action learning. (Adapted from Pearn and Kandola 1993:8)

Can such a wonderful organisation exist? The answer is yes. Learning organisations do exist, though only a few, and it is certainly within the capacity of every organisation to become one. Deep down, we are all learners. We all know, or remember, the excitement of acquiring formal knowledge, of learning from experience, of struggling through difficult times. We have all experienced the excitement of working with others to achieve important goals.

But many of us—over time and often without noticing—have lost our desire to learn and the behaviour that goes with it. We have picked up dysfunctional habits that prevent genuine learning. In relation to equal opportunities, instead of being effective learners, many of us have become 'snapshot thinkers': we label people, places and events; we no longer look for the connections or see, for example, the 'big picture' in which equal opportunities is about fundamental human issues rather than about British politics. Many of us have also become detached from the concerns that used to matter most to us, and have lost the vision of social justice and human fulfilment that used to inspire us. We have developed patterns of defensive behaviour which undermine genuine communication and team relationships. We shun genuine dialogue about the conflicting realities of equal opportunities, we avoid sharing our personal visions. We judge ourselves and others in terms of ideological purity. We want to be right and to be seen to be right

If such behaviour dominates the already difficult process of implementing equal opportunities, it is not surprising that few of us see this as an area in which we can exercise our creativity and continue to learn. Instead, many of us see equal opportunities as a necessary evil which we must survive defensively. The prospects for the continued development of genuine equal opportunities look grim.

What can we do then to stop our defensive habits and regain contact with our courage? How can we recapture our vision of a juster world? How can we ensure that the equal opportunities changes we have made so far will be maintained and developed? How can we turn our organisations into centres of equal opportunities creativity? We need to break the vicious circle by adopting new ways of behaving that promote genuine learning on equal opportunities. For each of us this means:

- scrutinising our mental models of equal opportunities;

- building a shared equal opportunities vision;

- encouraging and promoting team learning;

- thinking in terms of whole systems; and

- becoming more aware of our own behaviour, developing ourselves and facilitating development in others.

Each of these ideas is discussed in more detail in the rest of this chapter. Most of the material has been adapted from the work of Senge, who first developed and tested these methods of creating a learning organisation (Senge 1992).

Creating a learning organisation

Scrutinising our mental models of equal opportunities

Each of us carries within our subconscious deeply ingrained mental models—assumptions, generalisations, images, stories—which influence how we understand the world, what we see, and how we act. Many of these conflict with the ideas and values fundamental to equal opportunities. Because we are not normally aware of these mental models or their effects on us, they remain unexamined and so do not change. In order to change our established patterns of thinking and behaving in relation to equal opportunities, we need to bring our models to the surface, check them out and alter them where necessary. We need to embrace open dialogue on equal opportunities, abandon our defensive habits and risk the pain and threat of new information. We need to become committed to truth and to the best interests of people and of the organisation.

In our work with organisations, we have found few people who are genuinely open and committed to the search for truthful, accurate information on equal opportunities. Most people prefer half-pictures and closed arguments to the more complete but complex truth about discrimination and the equality movement. They also insist that only they and those who agree with them are right. In such a climate few people are brave enough to say what they really think.

For example, many people who actually find some of the ideas associated with equal opportunities confusing and difficult to understand, claim instead that they are totally committed and doing everything they can. They know it is unsafe to reveal their true views. They also know that if they do, other people are unlikely to ask, genuinely and openly, why they feel this way. In our advocacy of equal opportunities, most of us, when presented with a view that conflicts with our own, respond by strongly presenting our own view, leaving no space for genuine dialogue. We simply ignore the other person's mental model, missing a valuable opportunity to communicate properly with them and perhaps open their eyes to new ways of seeing things.

The next time you are at a meeting about equal opportunities, time how long it is until someone asks the first genuinely enquiring or exploratory question. It may easily be an hour or more. People are too busy stuffing each other with their own mental models of equal opportunities. But this only enables them to win arguments, not to find the best answer or the truth. Is it surprising that the more vehemently A argues about the oppressive nature of the organisation, the more threatened B feels, who does not think it is oppressive at all? So B argues back fiercely. And A counter-argues even more fiercely, and so on. People soon learn how gruelling this process is and avoid stating different or 'incorrect' beliefs in public. And we have all seen how such behaviour prevents learning and destroys working relationships, damaging individuals, teams and organisations.

Next time you find yourself arguing with other people about equal opportunities and get stuck, try to stop the escalating process in which you all simply force your mental models on each other. Ask a few simple questions in a genuine spirit of enquiry: What is it that leads you to feel that? Can you tell me why you have come to this conclusion? Can you illustrate your point so I can understand it better? By balancing your advocacy (belief in the complete unacceptability of discrimination in any form, and in the vital significance of equal opportunities) with your skills of enquiry (why and how have people developed such different models) you open both yourself and the other person to information that challenges your mental models and enables you to reconsider and refine them. We may need to accept, for example, that there are flaws in our own mental models, that mistakes were made in the way equal opportunities was introduced, or that our definition of discrimination needs amending. This is a small price to pay if we can also help other people open up and unblock their resistance to equal opportunities. And letting each other in on our own mental models helps move us towards developing a shared vision.

Building a shared equal opportunities vision

Vision is crucial in times of change. If people do not have a clear vision of where they need to go, they are reluctant to move away from where they are. But when they have a genuinely shared and positive equal opportunities vision which they are all committed to creating, they learn and move forward, not because they are told to, but because they want to. When people are working to achieve something that matters deeply to them they also become creative rather than adaptive learners.

Although there have been many wonderful *personal* equal opportunities visions in the past, few have been genuinely shared visions. Sometimes what has seemed to be a shared vision was in fact one person's vision to which other people had signed up. And when the equal opportunities programme ran inevitably into stormy waters— practical setbacks, loss of courage, doubts, failures of commitment— there was no shared over-arching vision to help steer the programme and keep it on course. A shared vision is vital, not a pleasant extra. It carries people through crises, holds them together and provides the focus and energy for them to keep learning. It gives people the courage and creativity to decide what they need to do, to experiment, and, if necessary, to learn from their mistakes, change direction and try again.

With the support of a shared equal opportunities vision, we also become more willing to expose and change deeply held views, and to recognise personal and organisational mistakes. Our colleagues are not asking for guarantees that every experiment will work. Everyone knows there can be no such guarantee. Nevertheless they remain committed. When an equal opportunities project fails, instead of pointing fingers of blame and defensively rejecting equal opportunities, people return to their shared vision. They have the courage and optimism to ask with open minds why it did not work.

People within an organisation need to spend time, formally and informally, refining and sharing their vision of equal opportunities. Everyone needs to understand the full meaning of equal opportunities and why it matters. Everyone needs chances to check out and modify their vision.

Encouraging and promoting team learning

When teams learn together they become amazingly effective. Most of those organisations that have implemented genuine equal opportunities successfully have done so through learning teams. But what makes a team learn?

First, the members must all want the same or similar results. Although this sounds obvious, in our experience it is more common for a team to be merely a group of individuals with different power bases, each with a different and 'superior' model of equal opportunities and each wanting different things. However hard people work in such a team, they waste vast amounts of energy and achieve very little. In contrast, a team which has taken the time to sort out its aims and vision, developing mutual trust and finding out what each member brings, achieves an extraordinary amount. Each person is empowered by and empowers the team. In the more common chaotic team, the empowerment of individuals merely increases the chaos and makes team management even more difficult.

Second, an effective team consciously cultivates the discipline of genuine dialogue, freely and openly exploring complex and difficult equal opportunities issues from many points of view, without game-playing or point-scoring, and giving members insights and understanding that they could not get alone. Many teams confuse dialogue and discussion. Discussion involves presenting and defending different views and searching for the best view to inform the decisions that must be made at the time. Dialogue is freer and more creative, explores more deeply, and involves listening completely while suspending one's own views. It does not necessarily lead to a decision. The two are potentially complementary, but many teams fail to distinguish between them, and stick mainly to discussion.

A team that has genuine dialogue on equal opportunities takes risks and engages in conflict in order to find a better solution. Provided it is handled constructively and sensitively, conflict over equal opportunities enables people to think more clearly and penetratingly and to build a firm consensus.

Third, an effective team cuts out 'defensive routines' (Argyris 1990). These are the habitual ways of interacting through which we protect both ourselves and others from threat or embarrassment, but which also prevent people from learning. Most of us find it frightening to expose our reasoning on equal opportunities in case people find errors in it.

Defensive routines are so numerous and so commonplace that they usually go unnoticed. If someone suggests beginning an equal opportunities project by putting everyone on a compulsory three-day awareness course, we may say 'That is a very interesting idea', when we know we disagree and have no intention of taking it seriously. We may avoid conflict by smoothing over differences or simply ignoring what people say, instead of asking them what lies behind their suggestion and then really listening. Alternatively, if we are angry with or dislike the person, we may confront them aggressively and argue them down, again avoiding considering the idea or the thinking behind it. Or we may protect other people and ourselves by saying nothing when it is clear that some of the information being presented is inaccurate. When a difficult issue comes up, we may change the subject to avoid unpleasantness. A team that practises these defensive routines cannot learn.

In a learning team the members take a decision to see, treat and trust each other as colleagues on a shared quest. They agree clear ground rules about communication and mutual behaviour. All this provides essential support and safety. Once equal opportunities 'adversaries' become simply equal opportunities 'colleagues with different views' we can allow other people to observe and question our assumptions, and can listen to their comments without jumping in to defend ourselves.

Unless teams can learn, the organisation cannot learn.

Thinking in terms of whole systems

Achieving successful and lasting change requires people to think in terms of whole systems and relationships rather than isolated parts, and to see changing patterns rather than static 'snapshots'. Systems thinking, which underlies this whole book, enables people to think strategically and to decide which interventions, carefully directed, will have maximum impact and are most likely to lead to significant and lasting change in relation to equal opportunities. The greatest leverage can often be obtained from relatively small but very well-focused interventions. Without systems thinking we often intervene in the wrong place, perhaps where the stress is most obvious. This often deals with symptoms rather than with real causes, providing short-term relief but no lasting change.

Systems thinking also means no longer seeing people as helpless reactors but as active participants in shaping their reality, no longer simply reacting to the present but creatively shaping the future. It means looking beyond complexity to underlying causes and structures. Complexity should not be ignored—unless the genuine complexity of equal opportunities is acknowledged and dealt with, people's confidence and commitment will be undermined—but should be organised into a coherent picture that illuminates the causes of problems and helps the development of lasting remedies. And, instead of ever more information, we need to know how to decide what is important and what is not, which factors to focus on and which to ignore. Learning to think in terms of systems takes practice.

Becoming more aware of our own behaviour, developing ourselves and facilitating development in others

Finally, in order to participate fully in developing and implementing equal opportunities, each of us needs to develop ourselves and to facilitate development in others. We need to work continually on clarifying and deepening our personal vision of equal opportunities, focusing our energy, being patient about the time it takes to see real results, and seeing things as they really are rather than through the spectacles of dogma. Although individual development on equal opportunities does not guarantee organisational development, there can be little organisational development on equal opportunities without it.

Surprisingly few organisations encourage genuine personal development. And very few people see themselves as developing and learning for the whole of their lives or as people who can help others to develop themselves. The result is vast untapped, unrecognised resources. Many people enter the equal opportunities change process bright, enthusiastic, and inquisitive, with high energy and a strong desire to make a difference. After a few years most of us lose our commitment, our sense of mission, and our enthusiasm. We no longer care whether vulnerable groups receive adequate services or unfair treatment, are ignored and marginalised, or are harassed and attacked. We are worn out and bored. We have spent so much time coping with the problems of the equal opportunities change process that we can no longer remember why we were on it in the first place. To avoid facing up to reality, we may pretend that things have improved in terms of equal opportunities and that the issues are no longer so urgent. We may develop a few defensive routines to cover our lack of vision and energy, and our failure to achieve results. At present only a tiny number of people involved in equal opportunities see themselves as developing and learning throughout their lives, and even fewer focus their energy on developing the skills necessary to spread the message and practice of equal opportunities.

No one can tell us how we should develop ourselves and what we should learn. Each of us must work out our own path. But the following passage from Senge, who uses the term personal mastery in this context, may give us a clue as to where to start:

'People with a high level of personal mastery share several basic characteristics. They have a special sense of purpose that lies behind their visions and goals. For such a person a vision is a calling rather than simply a good idea. They see "current reality" as an ally, not an enemy. They have learnt how to perceive and work with forces of change rather than resist those forces. They are deeply inquisitive, committed to continually seeing reality more and more accurately. They feel connected to others and to life itself. Yet they sacrifice none of their uniqueness. They feel as if they are part of a larger creative process which they can influence but cannot unilaterally control. People with a high level of personal mastery live in a continual learning mode. They never "arrive" .... They are acutely aware of their ignorance, their incompetence, their growth areas. And they are deeply self-confident.' (Senge 1992: 142)

Conclusion

Very few organisations yet possess the principles of true learning, or are able to support people through the thorny path to genuine equal opportunities. Without such support, the conflict and pain that are always involved in developing and implementing equal opportunities can become too much, shutting down the ability of individuals and organisations to learn, and killing many people's dreams and motivation. Some people have been driven to the more glamorous movement of diversity, which, though important, avoids confronting the ugliness and unacceptability of discrimination. The personal and organisational skills described in this book can help us get back on the right track and restore our integrity. We need urgently to learn these skills and to adopt those disciplines that will enable us and our organisations to push equal opportunities forward. There is no time to lose.

Appendix 1
Equal Opportunities Policy Statement from the Joseph Rowntree Charitable Trust

This statement covers the Joseph Rowntree Charitable Trust's three key areas of operation: decision making, grant making, and administration.

1. The Joseph Rowntree Charitable Trust is a Quaker trust and as such is rooted in a commitment to social justice, to non-violence and to respect for life. These values, whilst widely shared by others, are basic principles of the Religious Society of Friends (Quakers).

2. This commitment encompasses a belief in the equal worth of all members of the human race together with a recognition and appreciation of diversity.

3. The Trust recognises that certain groups and individuals in society are discriminated against on factors such as race, colour, gender, sexual orientation, religious affiliation, national origin, age and disability. It recognises that discrimination is embedded in our patterns of education, housing, employment, social interaction and political participation. These patterns are so pervasive that

frequently neither their perpetrators nor their victims realise when and how discriminatory acts are being committed.

4. The trust tries to promote equal opportunities in all aspects of its work. The main ways in which it aims to do this are through the measures outlined below.

a. Decision making

All trustees are members of the Society of Friends (London Yearly Meeting). Trustees are selected from within the society with a view to create a balance of perspectives and experience. A balance of ages and between men and women is sought. Trustees are aware that the Society of Friends is a small community which is not representative of the wider society to which it belongs. They are actively considering the issue of how a Quaker trust can effectively involve others in the decision making process. This is brought into focus when considering the Trust's relationship with ethnic minority communities. One way of addressing the matter has been to establish specialist committees comprising trustees and co-opted members. In relation to some of its work, the trust works through such committees and seeks to bring on to them persons in sympathy with the values of the trust who are involved and experienced in the issues on which the trust works. Through co-options the trust aims to broaden its perspectives and to include those who would not otherwise have the opportunity to participate. It believes that its decision making is enhanced through this process.

b. Administration

The trust staff is small and cannot reflect the various groups which make up the wider community. Staff recruitment is a rare occurrence but when openings become available the trust tries to create a balanced team and to ensure that no applicant is treated less favourably because of race, colour, gender, sexual orientation, national origin, age or disability. Selection criteria used and procedures adopted will be monitored for fairness.

So far as realistically possible, the trust aims to promote equality of opportunity with those with whom it enters into *contractual arrangements*. As a purchaser, the trust's small office has relatively little opportunity to exercise influence. However, in its investment programme, the trust aims to exercise ethical judgements, as it does in its grant making, and tries to use opportunities which are open to it to exercise influence over the policies of those companies in which it invests.

c. Grant making

The trust wishes to promote equal opportunities through its grant making programme. It wishes to encourage all applicants when applying for grants to consider this issue carefully. All proposals should include a paragraph indicating the applicants' approach to equal opportunities and how this will be reflected in the work to be funded. If an applicant considers this inappropriate the reasons for this should be indicated.

Depending on the nature of the project, the issues of equal opportunities is likely to be relevant to:

- planning and implementation processes
- management and staffing
- benefit or outcome.

The trust wishes to ensure that its grants are used in such a way that work funded does not exclude people on the grounds of race, colour, gender, sexual orientation, religious affiliation, national origin, age or disability.

A number of grants made by the trust are specifically designed to increase the participation of and equality for disadvantaged groups. The trust has a policy of supporting black and ethnic minority groups working within its fields of interest, subject to other criteria set out in the guidance notes for applicants.

5. This statement marks the beginning of a process for the Joseph Rowntree Charitable Trust. Trustees will keep the issue under review and monitor progress on a regular basis.

Appendix 2
Equal Opportunities Policy Statement from MCI (Management Charter Initiative)

This statement covers the four main areas of MCI's operation: marketing, development, networks and administration and finance.

I. Policy

1.1 MCI believes that equality of opportunity is socially, ethically and morally imperative. Furthermore, MCI recognises that progress towards equality of opportunity is progress towards its corporate mission—to improve the performance of UK organisations by improving the quality of UK managers. Organisations that use the principles and methods of equal opportunities will improve the quality and the diversity of appeal of their products and services, so that they reach a larger number and broader range of customers. This applies to MCI.

By adopting an equal opportunities policy MCI will improve its own performance.

1.2 Therefore MCI is committed to working towards equality of opportunity with the organisations through which it promotes its message, with its committees and within its own organisation.

1.3 As an employer and contractor, MCI will operate employment, selection and contracting procedures and practices based on a policy of merit alone which forbids discrimination for reasons of race, gender, disability, working patterns or sexual orientation.

2. Implementation

At corporate level this policy will be carried out by:

2.1 ensuring that MCI management standards, products and services are free from bias and cultural barriers as far as practicable and that equal opportunities is included as best management practice wherever appropriate;

2.2 working to remove the possibility of direct and indirect discrimination of groups or individuals arising from the practices and procedures of using the management standards including advice and assessment based on them;

2.3 ensuring that consultants and advisers used by MCI are qualified to give sound equal opportunities guidance and information;

2.4 seeking to work with organisations and individuals that operate to similar standards; and

2.5 treating all its employees and applicants for jobs equally.

At team level this policy will be carried out by:

Marketing

2.6 researching, designing, developing and distributing MCI products and services according to equal opportunities best practice;

2.7 whenever possible, ensuring that the MCI equal opportunities best practice standards are adhered to by our suppliers, agents and consultants; and

2.8 ensuring that all products and services are accessible to as wide and diverse an audience as possible.

Development

2.9 defining equal opportunity quality criteria against which all MCI products and services should be developed and evaluated;

2.10 ensuring that when selecting consultants, members of committees and steering groups, invitations are made to individuals from diverse backgrounds and cultures, and selected against predetermined criteria agreed by the administration director; and

2.11 ensuring that the management standards and other standards developed by MCI enshrine and reflect the principles of equal opportunities best practice in their content, language and structure.

Networks

2.12 promoting the MCI equal opportunities policy to network host organisations and encouraging them to adopt a similar policy, and to advise them of our experience and activities; and

2.13 advising MCI networks and other intermediaries to promote the ethical and business case for equal opportunities, and to advise how the management standards contribute to equal opportunities best practice.

Administration and finance

2.14 maintaining and monitoring a system where individuals are selected, promoted, and treated solely by their merit and abilities, based on predetermined selection criteria—which are appropriate to the job;

2.15 giving all employees equal opportunity and encouragement to progress within the organisation by carrying out the ongoing action programme;

2.16 providing training to improve individuals' prospects within the company and to enhance their understanding of the need for an equal opportunities programme;

2.17 encouraging employees who believe that they have been treated inequitably within the scope of this policy, to raise the matter as appropriate up to and including the formal grievance procedure;

2.18 meeting its legal obligations—both in spirit and to the letter of the law—under the Race Relations Act, the Equal Opportunities Act, the Equal Pay Act, the Disabled Persons Employment Act, and any other relevant legislation that is or may become current; and

2.19 distributing, explaining and publicising this policy statement throughout the organisation and elsewhere as is appropriate.

3. Monitoring

3.1 The Equal Opportunities Working Group is responsible to the chief executive for devising, implementing and updating the appropriate monitoring and evaluation systems to ensure this equal opportunities policy is carried out as intended.

3.2 The MCI executive is responsible for ensuring that this equal opportunities policy is followed and to deal with any actual or potential breaches.

27 October 1993

Appendix 3
Anti-racist Policy Statement and Code of Practice from Lambeth, Lewisham and Southwark Alcohol Counselling Service

The following policy statement was adopted by the management committee of the Alcohol Counselling Service—Lambeth, Lewisham and Southwark at its meeting on 13 July 1987. It is an essential part of ACS policy and the management committee expect that everyone in the organisation will implement and adhere to the action outlined in it and the accompanying code of practice, which explains in detail the implications of the policy.

1. We acknowledge the existence of racism and recognise the effects of white racism which affects our activities both as providers of services and as employers. We need to work to eliminate personal and institutional racism from the organisation.

2. Against this background the Alcohol Counselling Service aims to provide services to better meet the needs of black people and will regularly meet with black people in our community and ensure that their views have an influence upon the nature of the service.

3. To these ends we will identify and challenge racist attitudes, remarks and behaviour.

4. Our intention is that our counselling practices demonstrate a respect for and offer a welcome to black people as clients. We also intend to ensure that black people have equal access to our services. We need also to investigate whether counselling as we define it is an appropriate form of service delivery for different ethnic groups.

5. We will continue to take positive steps to increase the representation of black people at all levels of the service—management committee, staff, supervisors, voluntary counsellors and clients.

6. We will seek to ensure that no client, employee, voluntary counsellor, student, supervisor, or committee member receives less favourable treatment on the grounds of racial origin.

7. We will gradually review our programme of activities in the area of education and training to ensure that they reflect this anti-racist policy. This commitment to anti-racist practice will be made explicit to all those individuals, groups and organisations with whom we undertake education and training activities.

8. We will seek to combine this anti-racist policy with our long established practice and policy of highlighting gaps in service provision for people with alcohol-related problems. This will mean the need to concentrate on the lack of attention given to the needs of black people in all types of alcohol intervention and treatment.

9. We will endeavour to improve the levels of support in their work and opportunities for training that we offer to black people as employees, voluntary counsellors and students.

10. We will actively promote the development of anti-racist policies and practices on the part of agencies and organisations with whom we work.

11. In addition to the efforts to combat racism within the organisation as outlined above, members of staff, both black and white, should be allowed to spend 'reasonable' amounts of their working time addressing such issues at a more general level (at the discretion of the director) particularly with assisting agencies with whom we have a close working relationship.

12. We will regularly review this policy and practice throughout the organisation and will maintain a standing committee of the management committee to oversee this.

This anti-racist policy should be read in conjunction with the accompanying code of practice, guidelines and the ACS equal opportunities policy.

Code of Practice—Anti-racist Policy Statement

Item 1 We acknowledge the existence of racism and recognise the effects of white racism which affects our activities both as providers of services and employers. We need to work to eliminate personal and institutional racism from the organisation.

1. All people with alcohol-related problems and their families are disadvantaged by labelling, stigma and the low priority given to both statutory and voluntary efforts to help and treat them. Coupled with the effects of racism, black people in our community with alcohol-related problems and their families are therefore doubly disadvantaged. This must be acknowledged and its implications taken into account by all levels of the service.

2. The setting up and development of the service did not reflect the multiracial nature of the community in which

we are situated. Until fairly recently attention had not been given to developing strategies which would offer a service appropriate to the needs of local black people. Racist stereotypes of black people's drinking patterns were not vigorously or critically examined. The first steps that have now been taken in these directions must be continued and expanded.

3. In the past sole black workers have been employed and although the entire staff team at that time was much smaller the implications of this were not examined, or understood. Whether or not these were seen as token appointments is questionable but certainly the support needs of black workers in a white organisation were ignored. They were undoubtedly victims of both individual and organisational racism but in tribute to them they have all made considerable contributions to the service, and those no longer with us have progressed to very responsible positions. We must ensure that the strategies currently underway no longer allow these mistakes to happen.

4. The service has failed to develop and provide an atmosphere in which white committee members, staff and voluntary counsellors are encouraged to examine their personal racism. Despite lack of support, positive encouragement and direction from the top some white staff members and voluntary counsellors have taken the first steps in this direction. The management committee must both ensure that its own members pursue this themselves and that they provide the support and encouragement that staff and voluntary counsellors need to do so.

Item 2 The Alcohol Counselling Service aims to provide services to better meet the needs of black people and will regularly consult with black people in the community and ensure that the nature of the service is influenced by their views.

1. Last year a group of all the black people involved in the Service met and fed their views and needs to the management committee. Whilst this ad hoc group was a positive first step it now needs to be formalised as a standing committee which will be formally constituted, have clear terms of reference and feed directly to the management committee.

2. This Standing Anti-racist Management Group must be separate and not confused with the support needs of black people within the service. One or more separate support groups will need to be set up for black people within the service.

3. The service has developed some links with local black groups and organisations, eg Peckham Black Women's Group, but we need to both increase the number of such links and to devise strategies to ensure that their views have more impact on service policy and practice.

4. We need to devise strategies for regular formal consultation with black people in our community.

Item 3 ACS will identify and challenge racist attitudes, remarks and behaviour.

1. ACS as an employer, service and training agency recognises the deeply offensive nature and harmful effects of racist attitudes, remarks and behaviour. Such manifestations of racism are opposed to ACS's values and stated policies and therefore require identification and challenge whenever they occur in any ACS setting. There is a particular onus on white committee members and staff to make any necessary challenges and to do so whether or not black people are present.

2. Racist attitudes, remarks and behaviour can and do occur in a variety of forms ranging from the blatant to the subtle—the latter sometimes being in the form of anecdotes or 'jokes'. Despite their offensive and harmful effects it is important to acknowledge that these manifestations of racism are not always malicious in intent and may arise from a background of conditioning in a white racist society, lack of information and ignorance.

3. The predominant ethos and value systems of the service may tend to minimise the blatant malicious manifestations of racism but may also make it more difficult to recognise and challenge the subtle, unconscious racist attitudes, remarks and behaviour.

4. The form of challenges should at least in the first instance be in line with the usual values and practice of the service in that they should arise from a background of empathic understanding and use the principles of positive feedback. The service should continue and further develop training in recognising racist attitudes, remarks and behaviour and also training in 'How to challenge'.

5. Manifestations of racism can occur in a variety of settings and involving people at all levels of the service. The service should develop a set of clear guidelines for responding to them according to the setting and the level at which they arise, eg committee members, staff, voluntary counsellors, students and clients. These guidelines should clearly and specifically outline the process of recognition, challenge response and ultimate sanctions that should be applied if the former fail.

6. Given the nature of the service and its at times very difficult client group it is possible that one of the most difficult areas may concern the response to racist attitudes, remarks and behaviour from clients. It is likely therefore

that a special strategy will need to be developed to deal with such a situation. It may be that a special group of senior staff and supervisors needs to be established which would be called together to assist and support counsellors in dealing with this. The service policy should state clearly that if all else fails in such a situation it reserves the right to withdraw service from any client who continues to display racist attitudes, remarks or behaviour, and this policy should be made known to our funding bodies.

Item 4 Our intention is that our counselling practices demonstrate a respect for and offer a welcome to black people as clients. We also intend to ensure that black people have equal access to our services. We need also to investigate whether counselling as we define it is an appropriate form of service delivery for different ethnic groups.

1. We acknowledge that it is necessary to convey to potential black clients that they will be positively welcome in ACS circles. This welcome must be reflected in our literature, food and drink, decor and on the telephone.

2. To these ends immediate steps can be taken to ensure that black people do feel welcome in our premises. Racist graffiti if and when it occurs should be removed immediately. Photographs and posters should reflect our aspirations to become a multiracial agency. We should review our practice on the telephone and in reception of clients to ensure that this does not exclude black clients.

3. It should be recognised that some black clients may wish to exercise a choice in seeing a black counsellor. In order to make this choice possible we need to continue our efforts to recruit more black supervisors and voluntary counsellors and in the long term continue to seek mainline funding to employ more black full-time staff.

4. We need to continue to review our recruitment and selection procedures to ensure that they do not discriminate against black people and should establish regular intake training courses run by black staff for black people only.

Item 5 We will continue to take positive steps to increase the representation of black people at all levels of the service—management committee, staff, supervisors, voluntary counsellors and clients.

1. As for clients, items 4.1 and 4.2 will be equally important in providing a welcome to black people at all levels of the service.

2. Membership of the management committee could be encouraged both in the black community locally and by black people from outside the area who have special interest or expertise in areas affecting the service. The committee itself will need to consider ways in which it can attract black members and make them welcome and should emphasise the positive contribution that black people will make to the committee's future.

3. Efforts to increase the numbers of black staff members and voluntary counsellors should be continued and increased. This might mean the need to review our current practice in terms of publicity, recruitment and selection procedures and include the review of interviewing techniques and skills. These areas should be developed not as a 'special' sideline but as a part of the ACS's normal practice.

4. The current practice of offering black staff members and voluntary counsellors the choice of having a black supervisor must continue but it must be acknowledged that this might lead to a situation where the black staff members are 'overloaded'. The management committee needs therefore to consider a budget for paying external black supervisors on a sessional basis.

5. Current measures to produce publicity material aimed at the black/ethnic community must be encouraged and further developed but it is important also that all new publicity material mentions the needs of black people and reflects a multiracial approach to service provision.

Item 6 We will seek to ensure that no client, employee, voluntary counsellor, student, supervisor, or committee member receives less favourable treatment on the grounds of racial origin.

1. As for item 5.3 we must consider and adapt our practices for recruitment, selection, and training to reflect this policy and develop anti-racist interviewing techniques.

2. As outlined in item 3.5 a set of guidelines should be developed for dealing with incidents of racist attitudes, remarks and behaviour and whilst it is important to ensure that everyone is aware of these it is essential that particular efforts are taken to ensure that black people are aware of them.

3. Equally it is important that everyone is made aware of and understands clearly the ACS complaints procedure.

4. Again it is important to state the particular onus upon the white people involved in the service to implement this part of the policy.

Item 7 We will gradually review our programme of activities in the area of education and training to ensure that they reflect this anti-racist policy. This commitment to anti-racist practice will be made explicit to all those individuals, groups and organisations with whom we undertake education and training activities.

1. We should review our regular practices in education and training activities and seek to adapt them to ensure that they reflect a multiracial society.

2. Curriculum, exercises, case histories and other material should be gradually re-written to present positive images of black people.

3. A brief clear statement explaining these policies should be prepared and given to everyone attending any education event, training course, workshop, etc, and this should be an integral part of the informal contract which we have with other groups and organisations with whom we undertake training activities.

Item 8 We will seek to combine this anti-racist policy with our long established practice and policy of highlighting gaps in service provision for people with alcohol-related problems.

1. The majority of alcohol services do not reflect our multiracial society and do not consider the needs of black people in their service delivery. Many also do not consider the needs of other disadvantaged groups giving rise to a situation where, for example, black women and black lesbians and gay men are doubly disadvantaged.

2. There are factors we must take into consideration particularly when making referrals of black clients. The group approach used by many statutory and non-statutory services could lead to particular difficulties and too little attention has been given to the incidence of racism in such situations.

3. We should continue and increase the collecting of information on the working of alcohol services for black people. The majority of such services are based in North America and we need to find and develop links with bodies who co-ordinate such activities.

4. We must follow up and challenge any incidents of racism in other alcohol services as and when they are reported to us.

Item 9 We will endeavour to improve the levels of support in their work and opportunities for training that we offer to black people as employees, voluntary counsellors and students.

1. We should ensure that the support we offer to black employees, voluntary counsellors and students is adequate and appropriate and that they are given the time and space to meet their support needs.

2. The existing support group for black workers has only met on an informal basis and should be formalised and given more importance in the organisation.

3. We should continue and expand our policy of encouraging black workers both paid and voluntary to identify their training needs and also seek additional resources for funding this.

4. We need to spend some time discussing the advantages and disadvantages and therefore desirability of reserving some of our regular training events for black people only.

Item 10 and Item 11 We will actively promote the development of anti-racist policies and practices on the part of agencies and organisations with whom we work.

In addition to the efforts to combat racism within the organisation as outlined above, members of staff, both black and white, should be allowed to spend 'reasonable' amounts of their working time addressing such issues at a more general level (at the discretion of the director), particularly with assisting agencies with whom we have a close working relationship.

1. Both these two sections relate to the overall commitment in the service towards striving for an anti-racist community. We should both be encouraging others, particularly those with whom we work closely, to adopt similar strategies and policies and be open in sharing with them our experiences in this area both good and bad.

2. We should carefully monitor and record our experiences in developing these anti-racist policies and practices and be keen to share them with others. Possibly we could produce an information pack for similar organisations to ourselves. Our staff should be encouraged to write about our experiences and publish them.

Item 12   We will regularly review this policy and practice throughout the organisation and will maintain a standing committee of the management committee to oversee this.

1. A standing committee of the management committee should be established when this policy is approved and its membership, terms of reference, meetings, etc, should be clearly outlined.

Notes

Chapter 1

1. Discrimination through the conscious and unconscious norms, values and practices of organisations in all sectors resulting in the political, economic and social marginalisation or exclusion of minority groups.

Chapter 2

1. This is the name we use in this book. Many other names are possible including the equal opportunities working party, committee, team and so on. Choose a name that suits your organisation.

2. The board of trustees is the group of people who govern the charity and have ultimate legal responsibility for all the charity's activities. Your charity might use a different term such as executive committee, management committee, council, governing body or steering committee.

3. Used here to indicate members of all those groups listed in your organisation's equal opportunities policy.

Chapter 5

1. Deaf with a capital D is used within the Deaf community to refer to people who are profoundly or pre-lingually deaf and who use British sign language.

References

Argyris, C., *Overcoming Organisational Defences*, New York, Prentice Hall, 1990.

Burke, W.W., *Organisation Development: Principles and Practices*, Boston, Little, Brown and Co, 1982.

Commission for Racial Equality, *Code of Practice*, 1984.

Equal Opportunities Commission, *Code of Practice*, HMSO, 1985.

Garratt, B., *The Learning Organisation*, Fontana/Collins, 1987.

de Geus, A.P., 'Planning as Learning', *Harvard Business Review*, March-April 1988.

Handy, C., *Gods of Management: the Changing Work of Organisations*, Century Business, 1991.

Harrison, R., 'Choosing the Depth of Organisational Intervention', *Journal of Applied Behavioural Science*, 1970, Vol. 6, No. 2, pp. 181-207.

Kanter, R.M., *The Change Masters*, New York, Simon and Schuster, 1983.

Lewin, K., 'Group Decision and Social Change', pp. 197–211 in Maccolly, E.E., Newcomb, T.M. and Hartley, E.L. (eds), *Readings in Social Psychology*, New York, Holt, Rinehart and Winston, 1958.

Lippitt, R., Watson, J. and Westley, B., *Dynamics of Planned Change*, New York, Harcourt Brace, 1958.

Manpower Services Commission, *Code of Good Practice on the Employment of Disabled People*, 1984.

Mintzberg, H., *Structure in Fives: Designing Effective Organizations*, Prentice-Hall, Inc. 1983, p. 11.

Myers, C. and Davids, K., 'Knowing and Doing: Tacit Skills at Work', *Personnel Management*, February 1992.

Nadler, D.A. and Tushman, M.L. 'A Diagnostic Model for Organization Behaviour', in Hackman, J.R., Lawler, E.E. and Pinter, L.W. (eds), *Perspectives on Behavior in Organizations*, New York, McGraw Hill, 1977.

Nonaka, I, 'The Knowledge-Creating Company', *Harvard Business Review*, November–December 1991.

Pearce, J. and David, F., *Corporate Mission Statements: the Bottom Line*, Academy of Management Executive, 1987.

Pearn and Kandola, *A Toolkit for the Learning Organisation*, Oxford, 1993.

Peters, T., *Thriving on Chaos*, Pan Books in association with Macmillan, 1987.

Peters, T., *Liberation Management–Necessary Disorganisation for the Nanosecond Nineties*, Macmillan, 1992.

Political and Economic Planning, *Attitudes in British Management*, 1966.

Political and Economic Planning, *Racial Discrimination*, a report sponsored by Race Relations and the National Committee for Commonwealth Immigrants, 1967.

Rossi, Freeman and Wright, *Evaluation: a Systematic Approach*, Sage Publications, 1979.

Senge, P., *The Fifth Discipline: the Art and Practice of the Learning Organisation*, Century Business, 1992.

Stata, R., 'The Leader's New Work: Building Learning Organisations', *Sloan Management Review*, spring 1990.

Waterman, R.H., *The Renewal Factor*, New York, Bantam Books, 1987.

Further Reading

Equal opportunities

Brown, C., *Black and White Britain*, Heinemann, 1984.

Brown, C., *Racial Discrimination: Seventeen Years after the Act*, PSI, 1985.

Connelly, Naomi, *Ethnic Record Keeping and Monitoring in Service Delivery*, PSI, 1988.

CRE, *Code of Practice*, London, 1984.

CRE, *Why Keep Ethnic Records? (revised edition)*, London 1991.

EOC, *Code of Practice*, London, HMSO, 1985.

Manpower Services Commission, *Code of Good Practice on the Employment of Disabled People*, 1984.

Newnham, A., *Employment, Unemployment and Black People*, Runnymede Trust, 1986.

Palmer, Anya, *Less Equal than Others: a Survey of Lesbians and Gay Men at Work*, Stonewall, 1993.

RADAR, *Disability and Discrimination in Employment*, 1993.

Ross and Schneider, *From Equality to Diversity: a Business Case for Equal Opportunities*, London, Pitman, 1992.

Straw, J. *Equal Opportunities: the Way Ahead*, IPM, 1989.

Organisation development/change

Burke, W., *Organisation Development: Principles and Practices*, Boston, Little, Brown and Co, 1982.

Leigh, A., *Effective Change: Twenty Ways to Make It Happen*, London, IPM, 1988.

Williams, Dobson, Walters, *Changing Culture*, London, IPM, 1989.

Weiss, A., *Making It Work: Turning Strategy into Action Throughout Your Organisation*, Harper Business, 1990.

Evaluation

Hedley, R., *Measuring Success: a Guide to Evaluation for Voluntary and Community Groups*, London, Neighbourhood Care Action Programme, 1985.

Learning organisations

Argyris, C., *Overcoming Organisational Defences*, New York, Prentice-Hall, 1990.

Senge, P., *The Fifth Discipline: The Art and Practice of the Learning Organisation*, Century Business, 1992.

Understanding organisations

David, F., *Concepts of Strategic Management*, New York, MacMillan Publishing Co, 1993.

Handy, C., *Gods of Management: The Changing Work of Organisations*, Century Business, 1991.

Handy, C., *Understanding Voluntary Organisations*, Penguin, 1988.

NCVO Management Guides

Other titles in the series

Planning for the Future: An Introduction to Business Planning for Voluntary Organisations

Strategies for Success: A Self-help Guide to Strategic Planning for Voluntary Organisations

Surviving Working Together: The Art of Managing Complexity and Chaos (forthcoming)

Also available from NCVO Publications

Equal Opportunities and the Rural Voluntary Sector: 'Searching for a Needle in the Haystack'

Equal Opportunities in Voluntary Organisations (Reading List No 2)

Equal Opportunities Policies and the Rural Voluntary Sector: A Starter Pack

Fair Play in Rural Voluntary Organisations: A Guide to Equal Opportunities and Effective Working Practices

Investing in Black People: TECS and Black Communities—Meeting Local Needs

Making Opportunities: A Guide for Working Women and Their Employers

Supporting Black Voluntary Action: The Need for Black LDAs

Voluntary Sector Management Qualifications

If you want further details or a full stocklist please write to NCVO Publications. All orders should be sent to the following address:

NCVO Publications, Regent's Wharf, 8 All Saints Street, London N1 9RL, tel 071-713 6161, fax 071-713 6300.

Index